CONTENTS

THE ART AND CULTURE OF JAPAN

Nelly Delay

DISCOVERIES®
HARRY N. ABRAMS, INC., PUBLISHERS

A remarkable feature of Japanese civilization is the survival of primitive beliefs, associated with the country's rugged landscape. The Japanese have always had a fear of invisible forces and the deification of nature in the Shintō religion is a way of taming them.

CHAPTER 1

THE REALM OF THE 'KAMI'

The Japanese believe that they share the world with invisible forces, which they propitiate with offerings and magic rituals. The large red gates (*torii*) found all over Japan (the one opposite is in Miyajima Bay) are symbolic entrances to the supernatural world of the spirits (*kami*). Inari the fox (right) is the incarnation of one of these spirits.

Mythology

The myths and legends telling the story of the world's creation, the separation of heaven and earth, appear in two compilations that form the basis of Japanese culture: the *Kojiki*, 'Records of Ancient Matters', and the *Nihon Shoki*, a collection of official chronicles of the country's history.

In Japanese mythology three deities gave birth to seven generations of gods when heaven and earth were created. The last couple were called Izanagi and Izanami. Given the task of consolidating and fertilizing the earth, they viewed it from 'the Floating Bridge of Heaven' and then created water and islands. They had numerous offspring. When Izanami died, Izanagi was in despair. He wanted to go to the underworld to find his wife, but she refused to leave. Furious, Izanagi decided to return to earth. When he returned, he stripped naked and purified himself in the

The two rocks at Ise (below) look as though they have broken away from a single lump of rock. The space between them emphasizes that they were once joined. The Japanese believed that they represented Izanagi and Izanami, the couple in the creation myth. The rocks are permanently linked by a massive rope, a sign that they are both separate and united. It is one of the most striking examples of the harmony that exists in Japan between the solid and the void.

water, creating Amateratsu, goddess of the sun and light, Isukiyomi, the moon, queen of the night, and Susano-ō, ruler of the oceans.

One day the sun goddess, frightened by a violent altercation, fled to a grotto and sealed off the entrance with a huge stone. The gods were distraught. They conferred together but could not think of a way to bring Amateratsu out of the grotto. Suddenly the young Ama no Uzume, the goddess of laughter, started to dance. She placed necklaces of precious stones on the ground and a mirror outside the entrance to the grotto. Carried away by the rhythm of the dance, she gradually stripped off her clothes and then, completely naked, performed joyous and sensual movements with her feet. The gods all burst out laughing and Amateratsu, curious to know what all the noise was about, emerged from the grotto. Uzume told her that the gods were rejoicing because they had finally found a goddess more beautiful than she was. Amateratsu ventured out of the grotto and saw the jewels and

The Fuji goddess, Konohana Sakuya Hime (above), stands at the heart of the sacred mountain, halfway between the paths of the moon and the sun. The sun is a female deity, Amateratsu, depicted in red, the colour of the rising and setting sun.

the mirror reflecting her image. In a flash the god of strength closed up the grotto again and that was how light returned to the world for ever.

The Jōmon period (11,000 BC–300 BC)

The myth of the creation is timeless, but at the moment very little is known about Japan in the prehistoric period before 11,000 BC. The funerary jars and large ochre pots with intertwined patterns that have come down to us from the Jōmon period were made by the first tribes living on the islands of Ryūkyū and Hokkaidō. Carved and polished stones and pottery of increasingly intricate shapes and designs (some with rough drawings of the human figure) have been found deep underground. From these pieces it is possible to identify six subdivisions in the Jōmon period alone from which we can trace the development and movements of tribes that fell victim to volcanic eruptions and earthquakes.

It is clear from the subdivisions that there were at least two groups, one in the north and east, which came from Siberia via Sakhalin, and one in the south, probably from China and Korea. The harpoons, arrowheads, tooth-shaped jewelry and traces of sacrificial rituals suggest that the first group were the ancestors of the Ainu living in the north close to Siberia, who worshipped and sacrificed bears.

The Yayoi period (300 BC–AD 300)

In the Yayoi period the second group began leading a settled existence, growing rice,

Sea of Japan

Pacific Ocean

HOKKAIDO

Nemu

Sapporo

Hakodate

Aomori

Sendai

Niigata

HONSHU

Nikku ★

Edo (Tokyo)

Kanazawa

Yokohama

Mt Fuji ★

Kamakura

Nagoya

Mt Hiei ★

Heiankyo (Kyōto) ★

Kōbe

Nara

Ise

Osaka

Mt Koya ★

Hiroshima

Kita Kyushu

SHIKOKU

Nagasaki

KYUSHU

Kagoshima

★   Principal sites
▲   Prehistoric sites

0   60 km

0   40 miles

using wooden tools reinforced with iron and producing the first examples of weaving. Their dead were buried in huge urns with familiar objects around them, in the Chinese manner. A variety of bronze artefacts have been found, including mirrors, weapons and bracelets dating from the 1st century BC. Archaeologists have unearthed a large number of bells known as *dōtaku,* decorated with geometrical patterns and stylized human or animal figures. Their purpose has never been established, though it is possible that they were connected with agrarian rites or were used to seek protection from the gods.

Kuni, small states under a civil and religious leader (*shaman*), evolved over the centuries. As a result of the conflicts that broke out between these village states, some groups moved north to the Kinai region, later Yamato (the name given to Japan as a cultural entity). In the 1st century AD the *Hanshu,* which tells the story of the Han dynasty in China, mentions a country called Wa in the eastern sea.

This text can be viewed as the first written reference to clans or kingdoms that organized themselves under the mythical emperor Jimmu-Tenno and became Japan. The imperial dynasty probably evolved from one clan that became more powerful than the others. It

The terracotta jars from the Jōmon period (left) are imprinted with the marks of cords (*jōmon* in Japanese) attached to the top, the first known attempts at decoration. The bronze *dōtaku* (bottom left) date from the middle of the Yayoi period and were found buried on hilltops. They are particularly common on the island of Shikoku.

Opposite: map of the main sites in Japan.

The Ainu (above) were hunters and fishermen. They had their own unique physical characteristics: broad noses, prominent cheekbones, light complexions and very thick beards and hair. Their clothes were decorated with dark blue and white geometrical patterns.

traces its descent back to Ninigi, grandson of the red Amaterasu, goddess of the sun, and so has its roots in Japanese mythology.

The 'Tumulus' period

In the 3rd century AD leading members of clans began to have tombs built for themselves in the form of burial mounds, *kofun*, containing precious objects such as bronze mirrors, jade jewelry and iron swords. Stone or terracotta sarcophagi decorated with red ochre, blue and white painting are surrounded by *haniwa* ('circle of clay') sculptures of small houses, people and animals that accompany the dead person to the other world (presumably in place of the old sacrifices). The *haniwa* have a terracotta tube at the base so that they can be driven into the ground. They can justly be regarded as Japan's first sculptures, keeping watch over the valley of the shadows before the gods.

Shintō

Excavations have revealed very little about the religious beliefs of the early tribes. It was not until the 3rd century that a primitive form of Shintō began to emerge. Linked to rice cultivation, it initially had no rituals or places of worship, but sprang directly from myths and human life in symbiosis with nature. People's strength and fears come from nature and Shintō, which is an expression of that relationship, is bound up with the deepest roots of humanity. Over the centuries it has come to symbolize the identity and survival of the Japanese people, enabling them to come into contact with, and even assimilate, a whole range of religious or intellectual influences without losing their identity. Typhoons, volcanic eruptions and the power of rocks and water have always instilled in the Japanese the belief that the world has its own energy. People are part of the cosmos and have no individual existence separating

Large tombs or *kofun* (opposite) dating from the 3rd to the 7th centuries are found mainly in central and southern Japan. Over the centuries their shape changed and four identifiable types of *kofun* occur: *empun* (round), *hōfun* (square), *zempō-koen-fun* (keyhole) and *zempō-koho-fun* (square with a rectangle in front). Underneath the burial mounds, which delineate a sacred area, were one or two rooms in which the sarcophagi were placed. One wall of the burial chamber was decorated with black and red paintings on an ochre background, depicting scenes of everyday life – the first known paintings in Japanese civilization.

Haniwa terracotta sculptures (left) were placed in the tombs. Some have traces of different coloured pigments.

At Fushimi, near Kyōto, a complex of temples, *torii* and votive chapels is dedicated to the fox deity Inari and his messengers, the Kitsune foxes (left). The first buildings at this Shintō shrine were built in 711. Pilgrims go there to make wishes for prosperity and offerings to the stone statues of the fox deity, who wears a red bib as a symbol of his power.

them from the primal entity. Everything is part of the whole, the centre of energy. The void is simply fine matter, invisible to the human eye, in which links are created between the various components of the universe.

The visible and invisible are so closely interwoven that a whole mythology has grown up around the spirits, or *kami*, believed to live in plants, trees, stones and animals. These imaginary beings can be benevolent or malevolent and they are both feared and revered. Their presence is indicated by thick cords with vows and prayers attached to them. In Nara deer and hinds are consecrated and worshipped; one of the largest Shintō temples, in Fushimi, is dedicated to the fox Inari; and in Nachi it is the waterfall that is venerated.

In Fushimi (above) and elsewhere a straw cord twisted to the left is tied around the trunks of trees over a hundred years old, denoting their religious significance and the respect due to the spirits that live in them. The cords have pieces of white paper attached to them, addressed to the *kami* and folded ritually.

Kami

Since the 7th and 8th centuries innumerable Shintō gods have been worshipped. Offerings are made to them and ceremonies held at shrines and temples with unusually shaped roofs, designed to be in harmony with nature. Large bright-red *torii* (gates) stand at the temple entrances or in long rows stretching into the forest. Modest wooden structures dedicated to the local *kami* can even be seen in the fields and hills or by the roadside.

They are all part of daily life, playing a part in the festivals (*matsuri*) linked to agrarian rites. Every house has a Shintō altar where the spirits of the ancestors or family *kami* are worshipped and ritually offered rice, fruit or incense. To the Japanese the invisible world is just as real as the world in which we pass our transient lives. Any important occasion involves a Shintō ritual presided over by priests.

The Shintō priests serving the temples have a ritual rather than religious function. As messengers for humans and the *kami*, they perform purification rites with water, salt and rice. The priest (left) is wearing an *ema*, wooden plaques covered with votive paintings that gradually began to replace physical offerings to the spirits from the 10th century.

The temple of Ise Shimogo Jinja (below) is dedicated to the sun goddess Amateratsu and houses the sacred mirror, symbolizing the emperor's kinship with the sun. The thatched roof and interlaced exposed beams are typical of Shintō architecture.

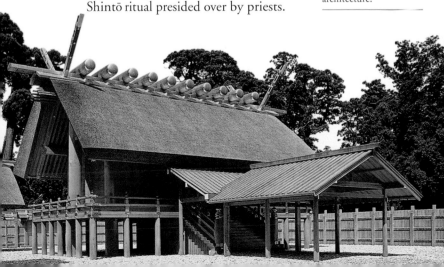

Shintō was already well established by 522, when emissaries from the Korean kingdom of Paekche brought a gilded bronze statue of the Buddha and sacred texts to the emperor of Japan as gifts. Frequent and violent internal clashes ensued between adherents of the two religions, until Prince Shōtoku Taishi declared Buddhism the state religion in 592.

CHAPTER 2

A BUDDHIST CIVILIZATION

Sākyamuni (right), a prince of Indian origin, became the founder of the new religion and was known as the Buddha. He has the same expression of human understanding and profound goodness on his face as Muchaku, a monk at the temple of Kōfuku-ji in Nara (opposite).

Buddhism comes to Japan

Buddhism originated in India and was brought to Japan via China and Korea in the 6th century by itinerant monks. After a period of conflict between Buddhism and Shintō a kind of synthesis was achieved, although Buddhism permeated all levels of society. Shintō, a link with the ancestors and the invisible forces in the world, was the predominant influence on all private and official occasions, but the rituals observed – the prayers and inner discipline leading to the 'Enlightenment' or 'state of the Buddha' – were Buddhist.

The first large Buddhist temple, the Hōkō-ji, was built in the 7th-century capital Asuka (near Nara), which lent its name to Japan's early period of history. At the time Japanese had no codified written language and the medium for the dissemination of Buddhism was Chinese. The *sutra*, the sacred texts containing the Buddha's teachings, helped to establish Chinese culture through the spoken and written

Opposite: the imperial prince Shōtoku Taishi (574–622; on the right), a scholarly man who was influenced by Chinese humanism and the sacred Buddhist texts, imposed Buddhism on Japan as the state religion, despite protests from traditionalists. His name is revered today at the Hōryū-ji temple in Nara.

The 7th-century masterpieces of statuary preserved at Hōryū-ji include the wooden statue of Kokuzo Bosatsu, the 'receptacle of space' Buddha (opposite right). Representing the universe as a matrix, he embraces all human beings in an equal and infinite love. With his hands he is making the *mudra*, a symbolic gesture of receiving and giving.

Many religious texts (left, a passage from the *Hoke-Kyō* or *Sutra of the Good Law*) were calligraphed on fans decorated with scenes of court life, linking the secular and the religious.

word and for a long time educated people and the upper classes used Chinese. All the major Chinese legal texts and literary works were also brought to Japan. Prince Shōtoku Taishi is believed to have drawn up the first Japanese constitution in Chinese around 604. It is both a moral code and a code of personal and social behaviour. 'Harmony is the most precious asset. We all alternate between wisdom and madness. It is a closed circle.'

Buddhism, which began as a political act when the prince made it the state religion, later cemented the relationship between the emperor, the nobility and the clergy and thus became a unifying force in Japanese society.

Nara, a political and religious capital

In the Shintō religion death was considered unclean and it was customary for the court to change its seat on the death of the emperor. His successor inaugurated his reign by building a new palace on an unsullied site.

That was how the court was established in Nara in 710. As well as the sanctuary reserved for the cult, all the leading noble families had temples built there, incorporating buildings for the study of doctrine and sacred texts, philosophy, science, the arts and the use of medicinal herbs as well as religious shrines. Several hundred monks gradually moved into temples and monasteries such as the Hōryū-ji (a few kilometres away), Kōfuku-ji, Tōshōdai-ji and Tōdai-ji. These communities (generally known as sects, a translation of the word *shu*) devoted themselves to spreading Buddhism through different but complementary teachings. The differences lay in their codes of ethics and esoteric initiations (for a small number of scholars) relating to the individual's place in space and time, based on the idea that the part and the whole are one.

Emperor Shōmu, who reigned in the 8th century, organized the country on the principle of an enormous *mandala*, a geometrical figure in which shapes and colours were arranged as a symbolic representation of the universe. The temple he

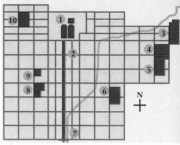

The new capital, Nara (plan above), was built on geometrical lines. Large temples were transferred there from the Asuka region and new buildings constructed entirely out of wood (below).
1. Imperial Palace
2. Red Phoenix Gate
3. Tōdai-ji
4. Kōfuku-ji
5. Gangō-ji
6. Daian-ji
7. Rajōmon Gate
8. Yakushi-ji
9. Tōshōdai-ji
10. Saidai-ji

Above: the Kōfuku-ji. Top to bottom: South Gate, Central Gate, shrine, lecture hall. Left and right: East and West Shrines. Beyond, on the right: five-storey tower. Left: South Pavilion. Bottom left: three-storey tower. Behind on the left: North Pavilion.

had built in Nara, the Tōdai-ji, was dedicated to the Buddha Vairocana and symbolized the universe in the centre of a lotus flower with a thousand petals. It is the largest wooden building in the world. At the same time millions of copies of the *sutra* and wood engravings of religious images were made for distribution to the pilgrims. They were the first printed documents in Japan.

The Tōdai-ji complex (plan above), was built in 743, burnt down in 1180 and rebuilt in the southern Chinese style. In 1567 the new building was also destroyed by fire, apart from the big Nandaimon Gate on the south side (opposite top). The third reconstruction, dating from 1688, is still standing today. The area of the building housing the Great Buddha was reduced by a third, without changing the height. Although this change made it slightly unbalanced, the scale is still just as impressive. The massive gilded bronze statue of Daibutsu (left), 16 metres (52 feet) high, was cast in 749 on the orders of the Emperor Shōmu. Resting on a lotus petal pedestal, it stands out against an 18th-century halo decorated with figures of the Buddha. The Tōdai-ji (opposite bottom) includes other buildings outside the walls of the main Dai Butsuden temple.

The Buddhist pantheon: an inspiration to artists

The Buddhist pantheon consists of an enormous number of Buddhas, bodhisattvas (deities who attend the Buddha on the road to Enlightenment), guardian kings (*myō-ō*) and gods of the underworld (*emma* and *oni*). In the 7th century they became the main source of inspiration for sculptors and painters, most of whom remained anonymous but achieved divine perfection in their works. The best-known Buddha, Amida, is the protector of the human race, taking it to the Western Paradise. He often appears behind mountains, his head bare, dressed in Indian-style clothes. He calls on heaven and earth to witness that he will not enter nirvana as long as there is just one person left to be saved. Dainichi Nyorai is the main

The Sanjūsangen-dō temple was built in Kyōto in 1164 on the orders of Emperor Goshizakana. It is also known as Rengeō-in or the temple of the thousand Kannons. One statue of Kannon with a thousand hands, made in cypress wood by the sculptor Tankei in the Kamakura period (1185–1333), has actually been preserved. The god is flanked by twenty-eight guardian gods in a room divided into thirty-three sections, with a thousand and one statues at his feet, each one different (below).

deity of the esoteric sects whose followers devoted themselves to the detailed study of doctrine. Fugen Bosatsu, the god of intelligence and compassion, understands the motivation of every human action and has the gift of prolonging life. He is portrayed sitting on a lotus resting on one or more white elephants and may have two or twenty arms. Kannon Bosatsu, one of Amida's two companions and the most revered bodhisattva in Japan, comes to the aid of all human beings. He appears in seven different forms: as Senju Kannon, surrounded by a halo of a thousand arms and forty hands, each with a symbolic attribute or making a *mudra* (a gesture with sacred meanings): as the six-armed Nyorin Kannon, sitting on a lotus; as the eleven-headed Ju-ichinren Kannon; as Sho Kannon the merciful, always at Dainichi's right hand; as Batō Kannon, with a horse's head, galloping to the four corners of the earth to come to the aid of the needy and chase out demons; and lastly as Jundu Kannon, with three eyes and eighteen arms, and Fuku-kensaku Kannon, god of the world of forms.

Fugen Bosatsu on his white elephant, coming from the east flanked by ten guards in a blaze of glory (above), is seen as the protector of followers of the *Lotus Sutra*. They had to recite the *sutra* and copy the text several times over (hence the large number of scrolls with *sutra* ideograms in gold ink on a blue background).

Miroku Bosatsu, the Buddha of the future, is especially revered. He will come down to earth five thousand six hundred and seventy million years after the Buddha enters nirvana and reveals the secrets of the Mahayana doctrines.

Jizō Bosatsu is the bodhisattva who intervenes in any situation to come to the aid of human beings. As the protector of children, he is especially venerated. He is always depicted as a young and handsome god, his face radiating serenity. Standing on an open lotus and dressed in a monk's robe, he holds the sacred jewels in one hand and in the other a pilgrim's staff, with rings that make a soothing sound.

Myōō and oni

Myōō are the messengers of the five chief Buddhas. Fudō, the most important myō-ō of all, is a manifestation of Dainichi Nyorai and is surrounded by flames representing his powers. In one hand he holds a sword to end life and in the other a rope to capture those who have transgressed the Buddha's law. Daitoku-Myōō, the most awesome embodiment of Amida, is also surrounded by flames. More powerful than a dragon, he conquered Emma-Hōō, king of the underworld. The other myōō are Kongo-Yasha, Gozanze and Gundari.

When Amida, the Buddha of light (below), comes to earth he will lead the faithful to the Pure Lands, paradise of the Buddhas and bodhisattvas. Those who have reached a certain level of Enlightenment by concentrating on the sacred formula *namu Amida butsu* ('surrender to the Buddha Amida') are delivered from ignorance and fear by Amida on his solar path.

In the 9th century the Shingon school introduced Fudō-Myōō (left), the king of science, appointed by the Buddha to vanquish the forces opposing Enlightenment. His body is painted dark blue, symbolizing self-control. The role of the god Jizō Bosatsu (below), the protector of children, is to unite the whole of humanity in infinite love and generosity.

Emma-Hōō is the supreme judge, but he only judges men. His sister decides the fate of women. Emma-Hōō is assisted by a number of demons (*oni*), which can take various forms and interfere in the world of the living but are not particularly dangerous.

Nara: the golden age of sculpture

The sculptures of the Nara period are the finest examples of the medium in Japan. The wooden statue of Miroku Bosatsu (opposite), one of the treasures of the Kōryū-ji, is regarded as an outstanding example of beauty and purity in Japanese art and is much revered. Miroku Bosatsu, also known as the bodhisattva Maitreya, is the 'Buddha of the future', the 'new saviour' who will lead people on the road to Enlightenment. In the Tōdai-ji temple the statue of Yakushi Nyorai, god of the Pure Land, is flanked by statues of his two assistants, Nikko, who transmits sunlight, and Gakko, who transmits moonlight (left). These 8th-century sculptures, over 2 metres (6 feet) high, are in polychrome clay, a major feat of artistry. The Buddha Yakushi Nyorai is also flanked by the 'guardian kings' Komokuten (p. 37) and Jikokuten (p. 36), clay sculptures about 1.60 metres (over 5 feet) high protecting the sacred area.

Representations of leading Japanese Buddhist monks like Saichō (767–822; meditating, below) or Kūkai (774–835; left) followed certain rules that enabled the faithful to recognize their faces and identify the symbols of their teachings. Numerous portraits of these monks existed as aids to meditation for monasteries and believers. Kūkai is depicted sitting on a lotus, holding in his right hand a *goko*, a symbolic object with a double trident, as an aid to contemplation of the inner self and the outer world. The statue of the monk Ganjin (opposite) was probably made in his lifetime and is greatly revered to this day.

Monks venerated like gods

The most eminent monks, the founders of schools and sects, are portrayed in sculptures or paintings placed in temples and monasteries either to help the monks to meditate or to be venerated by pilgrims, who often take reproductions of the portraits home for their domestic altars.

Six schools of Buddhist teaching developed in Nara in the 8th century. Based on Indian Sanskrit texts and *sutra* calligraphed by the monks and Japanese scholars

in classical Chinese, they spread
the study of consciousness and
knowledge. The Ritsu school,
one of the best known, was
founded in 754 by a Chinese
monk who took the name
Ganjin. He recited the *sutra*
by heart after going blind.

Another monk, Saichō
(who later took the name
Dengyō Daishi) was
renowned as teacher of
doctrine. Initiated into the
doctrine of the Hossō school
at the age of fourteen, he
studied the teachings of
the Chinese masters, in
particular the *Lotus Sutra*,
one of the most sacred
Buddhist prayers.
In 794 he founded a
monastery near Kyōto, later
named Enryaku-ji, which
became the headquarters of the
Tendai school. Saichō had studied
the precepts of the 'True Word'
and tried to pass on the Buddha's
teaching without obscuring it by
interpretation.

The invention of Japanese script

A monk called Kūkai, later Kōbō
Daishi, went to China to follow the
teaching of the 'True Word' at the
beginning of the 9th century. When he returned
to Japan a few years later he brought back not only
sacred objects but also a fund of knowledge that
he tried to pass on.

In 816 he founded the Kongōbu-ji temple on
Mount Kōya, south of Kyōto, and turned it

The esoteric Shingon school taught the *mantra*, secret words, the *mudra*, the symbolism of gestures, and the reading of the *mandala*, a symbolic representation of the world. The *mandala* to the left is based on the number five. The name of a deity is written in Sanskrit in each of the squares or circles. It could only be deciphered by the initiated.

The two *nyō* guards (below) stand on either side of the south door of the Tōdai-ji. According to legend, the two massive statues, over 8 metres (26 feet) tall, were made by Kei masters in less than two months.

into a centre for Shingon, a leading esoteric Buddhist sect devoted entirely to the study of the sacred texts.

Kūkai invented the *kana* characters, the syllabic symbols from which Japanese script evolved, based on the esoteric script derived from Sanskrit. He wrote a poem in which each symbol appeared only once, a poetic expression of the characteristically Buddhist concept of the impermanence of the visible world. Kūkai circulated various tracts, including one on the Ten Stations of Thought and another on The

Universe of Consciousness, expounding the idea that the real world that people are experiencing here and now is the supreme reality which it is essential to try to understand.

Artist monks

The portraits of leaders of the major sects, the pictures of the gods and the other legendary Buddhist scenes are all unsigned. The artists left no trace of their names and were most probably monks working in monasteries.

Unlike the painters, a few of the major sculptors attached to famous temples and monasteries did identify themselves and some of the world's art treasures can be reliably attributed to them.

In 1199 the monk Chōgen completed the restoration of the Tōdai-ji and Kōfuku-ji temples in Nara, burned down by the Taira clan, who left the city after being defeated. Yorimoto, head of the victorious Minamoto clan, decided to restore the temples as a gesture of gratitude to the soldier monks who had supported him in the war. He called in artists from the Kei school founded by the sculptor Kōkei.

In 1203 Kōkei's son Unkei and his pupil Kaikei made two monumental wooden sculptures of nyō (door-keepers) for the Tōdai-ji. For the Kōfuku-ji temple they made two statues representing Seshin and Muchaku, disciples of the Buddha Miroku.

Kūkai invented the first Japanese script with bold brushstrokes known as *hikaku* (above), using Sanskrit characters as his model. Some of his manuscripts, dating from the late 9th century, are still preserved in the monastery of Koya-san, headquarters of the Shingon school.

In 794 Emperor Kammu decided to leave Nara and build a new capital to escape from the influence of the monks. The city (now Kyōto) was named Heiankyō, 'the place of peace and purity'. The Heian period is regarded as the golden age of Japanese civilization. In the 15th century it inspired the dazzling Momoyama Renaissance and it remained the cultural model for the nobility until the 18th century.

CHAPTER 3
THE ART OF THE COURT

Falconry was a popular court pastime. In the 16th century magnificently attired princes and dignitaries inspired the painters of the Tosa school (opposite) in the Momoyama period. During the Renaissance Kōrin designed precious objects (right, a writing case).

The court and noble families had lavish temples and religious establishments built as symbols of their power. At the Byōdō-in in Heiankyō, built by the minister Minamoto no Toru in 1052, all the buildings, particularly the Phoenix Hall (Hōō-dō) dedicated to Amida, were designed to create an impression of magnificence modelled on the description of the Paradise of the Pure Land by the monk Genshin (942–1017) in *Ojū Yōshū (What is Essential for Rebirth in the Pure Land)*, where the afterlife is of such perfect beauty that it makes death almost desirable. In the Hōōdō is a statue of the Buddha Amida by Jōchō (c. 1053), over two metres (6 feet) high and entirely covered in gold. Hollow sculptures like these, assembled from pieces of wood, have been found to contain temple treasures such as gold-painted *sutra* on a dark-blue background, fine pearls and precious objects.

Life at court

In the Heian period (794–1185), the nobles lived in a harmonious and sophisticated way. The vast rooms in their palaces were full of paintings with the colours

• It had rained for days without stopping and a few drops were still falling when the moon appeared in the brilliant sky. On the way the prince passed close to a deserted tumbledown house overgrown with vegetation of all kinds. The wormwood had grown so thick that it was impossible even to see what the house used to be like. The rain was still falling through the branches. Koremitsu sheltered the prince with his umbrella. •

Genji monogatari,
Book 15,
Chapter 3, 'The
Wormwood
House'

picked out in gold leaf, a magnificent setting befitting an emperor's entourage.

The nobles spent their time on trivial activities that assumed great importance in the luxurious ambience of the court: playing with perfumes and shells, poetry and calligraphy competitions, ball-games (*kemari*), walks to admire the first flowers, flute lessons. The courtiers did not see their lives as futile; on the contrary, each minute detail was appreciated to the full and they felt a kind of melancholy at the fragility and transience of life. The feeling that life was fleeting was originally a Buddhist idea. In the Heian period more importance was attached to aesthetics than to ethics. The courtiers knew nothing about the scientific discoveries in China or the work on human behaviour in esoteric Buddhism, or indeed the famines and poverty in the rest of the country.

The Byōdō-in at Uji, near Kyōto, was originally a villa owned by the powerful Fujiwara family. The Hōō-dō or Phoenix Hall (left), jutting out over an irregularly shaped lake strewn with lotus flowers, was converted to a monastery around 1052 to house the famous sculpture of Amida Nyorai, Saviour of the Western Paradise of the Pure Land (above). The only statue of this kind still intact, the Buddha Amida in a position of meditation surrounded by bodhisattvas, is the work of the sculptor Jōchō, who influenced all the religious statuary of his day.

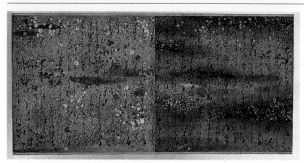

Transcribers have made numerous copies of the *Genji monogatari* (left). It was always written on fine paper, highlighted in silver and gold.

Women's language and literature

The *kana* characters invented by the monk Kūkai had unexpected effects on culture. Upper-class women in the Heian period adopted the everyday language and used the new script to write the first novels in Japanese. Monks, diplomats and scientists continued to write in Chinese, which they considered more elegant, but it was seen as bad form for women to use Chinese. The female courtiers, living in confinement in the palace and restricted by the rigid etiquette and their sumptuous kimonos, observed very closely what was going on amongst the nobles and servants. They skilfully interpreted the intrigues that they saw and recounted them in texts full of subtlety and poetry.

In the early 11th century Lady Murasaki Shikibu wrote *Genji monagatari (The Tale of Genji)*, chronicling the life and loves of the Shining Prince, based on the heir to the throne. This immense work in fifty-four chapters is the supreme masterpiece of Japanese literature.

It soon became an inspiration for painters in the *Edokoro*, a sort of government-run academy. They illustrated the main scenes on scrolls on which calligraphy alternated with pictures, to be read out loud at court.

In the 11th century other noblewomen followed Murasaki Shikibu's example, writing travel diaries like Sarashina or the witty *Pillow Book* like Lady Sei Shōnagon.

The first paintings inspired by the world of the *Genji*, known as *onna-e* (women's paintings), appeared a century after the text itself, in the Heian period and the 16th-century Renaissance. The portrait of a female poet (below), sitting in front of her writing case next to a lamp, recalls a passage in the *Genji*: 'She began corresponding with the prince, with many precautions and subterfuges. Genji was only too well aware of the fatal consequences of indiscretion.'

The first series of illustrated scrolls of the *Genji* must originally have comprised ninety scenes, divided into fifty-four chapters. Only nineteen scenes have been preserved, in thirteen chapters. From the copies that have been made it is still possible to transcribe the text in full. The subjects of the paintings re-create the poetic atmosphere of the setting and the feeling of nostalgia. The interplay between the oblique lines of the architecture and the geometrical patterns of the clothes creates an impression of animation. The hats worn by the nobles are like musical notes in the space. The eye is drawn into the composition and the 'open roof' technique provides an aerial view and alters the perspective.

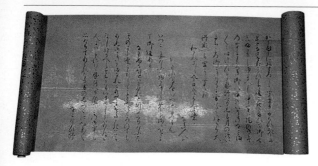

E*maki* are unrolled in the direction of the text, section by section, each section measuring the normal distance between the arms. At court they were read out loud, with everyone admiring and commenting on the illustrations.

A hedonistic court

After the emperor Go-Ichijo had redistributed posts between the various noble families, a number of different factions grew up, all vying for supremacy. The Fujiwara soon began to gain ascendancy over the imperial family, controlling affairs of state and cultural life. They transformed life at court and fostered a cult of beauty.

Artists and craftsmen flocked to the Fujiwara court, where both had equal status. To satisfy the demands of their patrons, they created patterns for precious silks woven with gold and silver thread. They skilfully fashioned wood and gold, sometimes pearl-encrusted, into chests or bookshelves with carved bronze corners. The paintings often incorporated still life, illustrating the magnificent objects in daily use, such as writing desks, richly decorated musical instruments like the *biwa* and *koto*, bronze mirrors and screens with gold backgrounds.

The art of the *emaki*

The *emaki* is a hand scroll with paintings and calligraphy, read horizontally from right to left. The first example was probably the *Genji monogatari*, painted in the early part of the 12th century when

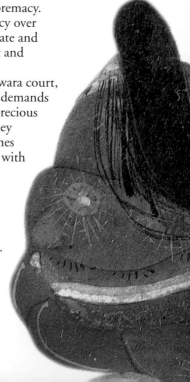

it became the fashion for painters and calligraphers to work together. The complementary text and illustrations had a profound influence on secular and Buddhist painting in Japan.

Over the next few centuries *emaki* began to incorporate completely new subjects: natural disasters (such as floods and fires), ghosts and devils, nature and architecture and in particular servants and working-class figures mingling with the aristocracy.

Emaki painting continued to evolve for the next few centuries, providing an artistic record of court and everyday life. By comparing and crosschecking buildings, sculptures and gardens, for instance, can be dated fairly accurately from these first-hand observations. Because of their shape and the way in which they are unrolled *emaki* have to be composed in a very specific style, but the harmonization of the colours places them in the general tradition of pictorial art. *Emaki* can be almost nine metres (30 feet) long and it took considerable technical skill to stick the sheets of paper between them. Some that were

Trompe l'oeil bookcases, books and writing cases (below) feature in many paintings.

The mysterious silhouette of a woman seen from behind is a recurring motif in Japanese erotic art (left). A seductive and artistic effect is created by the long flowing black tresses hanging down to the hem of the silk kimono, which is in subtle harmonizing colours. She is the quintessence of the mysterious woman whom Prince Genji pursued in his dreams.

made for rich art connoisseurs are still famous, for instance *Shigisan engi emaki (Legends of Mount Shigi)* dating from around 1160, *Kibi Daijin Nitto emaki (The Adventures of Minister Kibi in China)* and especially *Chōjū giga emaki (Satirical History of Birds and Animals)* attributed to Kakuyū, known as Toba Sōjō (1053–1140). This series is regarded as one of the masterpieces of Japanese art and has inspired numerous painters of metamorphosis and anthropomorphism.

Toba Sōjō painted animals engaged in human activities. He produced one of the most famous 12th-century *emaki* (below), beautifully drawn and full of humour. In the land of the Shintō religion it seems natural to make no distinction between humans and animals.

In this 16th-century *emaki* by Sumiyoshi Gukei (left), Prince Genji is leaning on the *engawa* (veranda) of his palace, looking at the Chinese stones in the nearby lake that are reminiscent of famous landscapes. The *Sakuteiki* (*The Secret Book of Gardens*), another illustrated 16th-century text, refers to the *kami* spirits living in the stones. The function of the stones was to protect palaces and shrines. Their shape, the way they were arranged, the colours and types of plants were governed by very strict rules.

Palaces and early gardens

In the Heian period the aristocracy built palaces modelled on the Paradise described by the Buddha Amida. The choice of site was crucial. The architecture embraced all the arts: the planning of a space linking indoors and outdoors, painting and sculpture. It was the first time that gardens had been designed to re-create nature. Nothing remains of them now, but there are allusions to them in the *Genji monogatari* and the paintings it inspired. The artificial lake is a central feature. Projecting from the water are hollow irregular rocks that have a symbolic meaning. Their shape is reminiscent of famous landscapes in China, or they might be arranged like esoteric figures or suggest islands, waterfalls and streams. A variety of species is used to make the landscape look as natural as possible.

Some of the Heian gardens are embellished with flowers such as

Above and below: flowers in a Heian garden, illustrations for *Genji monogatari*.

carnations, peonies, chrysanthemums, campanulas and lespedezas, in carefully coordinated colours. Shaped pine trees grow next to maples and *sanaki* (similar to a camellia), sometimes with plum trees, the first to flower in the spring.

Buddhist influence

The gardens were designed to be viewed from wooden verandas, *engawa*, around the buildings, performing one of the main functions of architecture, which is to link indoors and outdoors. The effects of reflections, transparency and space-time relationships echo the Buddhist view of the world. The art of the garden has close and complex links not only with Buddhism but also with Shintō, in which the trees, rocks and water where the invisible *kami* spirits live are venerated.

The gardens are outstanding examples of Japanese aesthetics and ethics. A number of works have been written about their design and symbolism, discussing the methods and rituals to be observed in their creation. The first was the 12th-century *Sakutei-ki* (*The Secret Book of Gardens*), inspired by the real or legendary landscapes of the old Japanese myths and providing a key to deciphering the ethical and

Shūgaku-in (below), an imperial villa north of Kyōto, is surrounded by gardens that rearrange nature. This is the first example of a landscaped garden.

aesthetic meaning of the art of gardens. It was followed in the 15th century by the *Sanzui Narabini yagyō no zu* (*Landscape and Countryside Drawings*), illustrated by sketches and literary and poetic observations.

The Momoyama period

The art of the Heian period inspired a brief Japanese Renaissance in the Momoyama period from 1573 to 1615. Momoyama (meaning 'the peach tree hill') was the name of the place south of Kyōto surrounded by peach trees where Toyotomi Hideyoshi (1536–98) built the castle of Fushimi.

After a long period of civil war and conflict between factions from the 12th to the 16th centuries, the warlord Oda Nobunaga (1534–82) seized power from the Ashikaga clan and established himself as ruler. In this period the country was ruled by three leading warlords in succession: Nobunaga, Hideyoshi and Tokugawa Ieyasu (1542–1616). To consolidate their positions and give themselves

In the 16th century, monastery and palace architecture obeyed the same principles: strict rules, simple and natural materials (opposite).

In the stately residences the living areas were made up of a series of different-sized sections (above) linked by open or closed galleries, creating a homogeneous whole that was integrated with parts of the large garden surrounding the building. Partitions between the interior and exterior could be moved around in different lights or seasons.

roots and legitimacy, Japan's new rulers had palaces and fortresses built in the Heian style.

Katsura Rikyū

The 17th-century villa built at Katsura, south of Arashiyama near what is now Kyōto, is regarded as a masterpiece of elegance, harmony and symbolism.

The imperial prince Toshihito (1579–1629) was a devotee of the *Genji monogatari*, with its descriptions of the palaces and gardens frequented by Prince Genji and Princess Akashi. It inspired him in 1624 to start building a house surrounded by a garden where the court scholars and poets could meet. More buildings were added, the gardens were extended and the 'House in a Melon Field' on the banks of the river Katsura gradually became the imperial summer residence. The construction was supervised by Enshu (1579–1647), applying the principles of perfect harmony in which a building has to be integrated into its natural environment. Five pavilions used as meeting places for poets or for the tea ceremony stand around a lake with three islands in it, arranged according to the principles in the *Sakutei-ki*. Each pavilion looks out on to a different landscape that is coordinated with the interior decor.

Katsura Rikyū is a fundamental link between palace and monastery gardens and poets' retreats. The imperial villa, designed on traditional lines, established aesthetic standards that later influenced Japanese architecture for many centuries.

The imperial villa, the Katsura Rikyū, is an outstanding example of Japanese architecture. Its geometrical simplicity is emphasized by the white of the *shoji* alternating with the dark brown of the wood (bottom right). The whole building seems to be almost floating on its piles. The irregular overhang on to the garden lends variety to the facade (bottom left). One of the rooms adjoined the 'moonlight terrace' (*tsukimidai*), so called because from this point the finest view was over the garden at night. Shade is important in the villa's interior rooms. The *shoji* could be opened wide on to the garden or kept closed for a pale indoor light. The waters of the lake (above left), designed according to the principles of *The Secret Book of Gardens*, were scattered with stones that had a symbolic meaning and were arranged according to strict rules. The bridges across the narrow parts of the lake were designed to be seen from different angles, breaking the monotony of the water.

Decor and painting

The decor of the huge residences (painted partitions, screens with gold backgrounds) and the design of precious objects was ostentatiously lavish. Two artists were instrumental in reviving the splendours of the Heian period described in the *Genji monogatari* and illustrated in the *emaki* pictures: the painter Tawayara Sōtatsu (c. 1570–1640) and a brilliant calligrapher called Honami Kōetsu (1558–1637). Working together, they gathered a number of other artists around them in Kōetsu's village, including the calligrapher Mitsuhiro and the tea master and garden designer Kobori Enshu. In the 16th century another artistic movement developed around Tosa Mitsuyoshi

The subjects illustrated on screens created an illusion of space in the rooms, which were next to the real space of the gardens (below, flowers in the Kanō style).

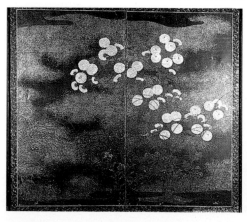

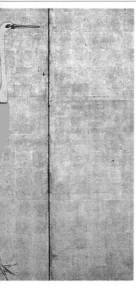

(c. 1536–1613), with the backing of the court academy of painting *(Edokoro)*. This colourful and harmonious new style, often embellished with gold clouds, was called Tosa. It was kept alive by a dynasty of painters until the 19th century.

After Tosa Mitsuyoshi and Tosa Mitsunobu the 16th-century artists took their inspiration from the Heian *emaki* scrolls and tried to revive the Yamato spirit that inspired the *Genji monogatari,* the *Ise monogatari (Tales of Ise)* and the *Saigyō monogatari (The Story of Saigyō the Monk).*

At the same time Kanō Motonobu founded the Kanō school. It was initially based on the ink paintings that were a legacy of Chinese philosophy, but the later works, huge and colourful compositions with flowers, trees and birds on a gold background, reflected the magnificence of the age. In the 17th century the tradition was followed by Ogata Kōrin, regarded as the greatest of the Japanese designers, who produced compositions in a sweeping and austere style for partitions and screens and also fans, lacquer cabinets, combs and *inros* (medicine boxes with compartments), using gold, lead and mother-of-pearl with great artistry. Kanō Eitoku, who also decorated palaces, worked mainly in ink but sometimes used gold and harmoniously blended colours that were fashionable at the time.

In the Momoyama period the decorative arts flourished. Powdered eggshell was mixed with mineral and vegetable pigments to produce a kind of relief making the colours more brilliant. Lacquer was used to add gloss to the black and lend a trompe l'oeil effect to the objects portrayed (overleaf, bookcases). Ogata Kōrin's works (left) were noted for their bold composition and vigorous style.

Below: calligraphy from the *Genji* by the painter Honami Kōetsu.

The only scenery in the quasi-religious *Nō* theatre is the ancient cypress at the back of the stage (left). The rest is left to the audience's imagination.

Nō theatre

Nō theatre, a noble and religious form of theatre invented by the actor Zeami (1363–1443), was first performed at court and in temples in the 15th century. The chanted words, mixed with singing and very slow movements, are a formalized tragic ritual. *Nō* derives from the old religious dances performed outside temples such as the *gigaku*, the *bunraku* and the *gagaku*, in which the rhythmic musical accompaniment interacted with the inflexions of the actors' voices, without the aid of any text. The actors wore masks representing demons, legendary animals and foreign or mythical figures.

Nō actors also wear masks, particularly the *shite* or leading character who is partnered by the unmasked *waki*. There are various kinds of mask; they might, for instance, represent women, young princes, drunkards, ogresses or demons. The action is always played out between the real and the supernatural worlds. The stage on which this fantastic encounter takes place is square and the scenery minimal: light-coloured cypresses, with a 'mirror partition' at the back, decorated with an old pine tree with heavy green branches.

The musicians are on a dais on the right. The wings and stage are linked by a gangway 8 to 12 metres (26 to 39 feet) long.

The curtain suddenly opens, there is a shrill burst on the flute and the *shite* appears. *Nō* theatre is essentially magical. Just as in opera, the words are a medium. Everything is expressed by sound (voices or instruments), the different pace of the actors' movements, the play of light on the masks which makes them come alive. The distortion of time and sound and the lighting create an unreal setting for the supernatural. After Zeami established the basic principles of *Nō* in the 15th century, it became very popular with the court and warriors. Since the 17th century it has had a more formalized structure, but it has retained its timeless and magical spirit.

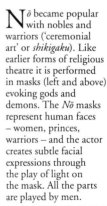

Nō became popular with nobles and warriors ('ceremonial art' or *shikigaku*). Like earlier forms of religious theatre it is performed in masks (left and above) evoking gods and demons. The *Nō* masks represent human faces – women, princes, warriors – and the actor creates subtle facial expressions through the play of light on the mask. All the parts are played by men.

In the old days Japan was made up of small rival states that were almost permanently at war. Soldiers recruited by the nobility set themselves up as a caste enjoying special privileges. Known as the *samurai*, they established a code of honour for themselves, *bushidō*, governing their conduct in war and their spiritual life.

CHAPTER 4
THE WAY OF THE WARRIOR

The fan (*ogi*), part of the insignia of command carried by generals, had a blazon on it (right), with the red sun on one side and the moon on the other. Each warrior fought under the coat of arms of a clan.

Opposite: the capture of Osaka.

The warrior caste

By around 900 the central government was proving incapable of keeping order in the country and coping with the famines. Rich provincial landowners set up and maintained their own private armies, arming and organizing groups of warriors to defend their estates. In the conflicts over land ownership these armies became increasingly large and powerful. At the same time the nobles were tightening their hold over the emperor, to the point where he was no longer in effective control of the country. In their struggle for power they conferred a special status on the powerful warrior caste.

From the 12th century onwards warriors (*bushi* or *samurai*) were the highest of the four castes in Japan's

In the 11th century warriors adopted the *ōyoroi*, a suit of armour made of long articulated iron plates lined with leather, and tall horned helmets, *hoshi kabuto*. Opposite: an archer holding the horsehide *saikai*, part of the insignia of command. The Japanese later made films of the *samurai* epics (above, a scene from Kurosawa's *Kagemusha* of 1980).

social hierarchy, warriors, peasants, artisans and tradesmen. The *samurai* were subject to the nobility and owed absolute allegiance to their lord (*daimyō*). Individually they obeyed a code of honour or ethics, *bushidō*, the Way of the Warrior, laying down rules for conduct in battle based on inner discipline and governing relationships between members of the same group or family and their subordination to a lord. They lived simply and frugally. It was their duty to show solidarity, honour and gallantry in battle.

In the 18th century forty-seven faithful vassals (*rōnin* or 'unemployed warriors') attacked Kira castle to avenge their master Asano Naganori. After their victory they were sentenced to *seppuku*, ritual suicide. This episode inspired the most famous *Kabuki* play, *Chushingura*, written by Chikamatsu Monzaemon and illustrated by Kuniyoshi (left).

Their lives belonged to their lord and they had an obligation to avenge him. The *Tale of the Forty-seven Ronin* (1703) is the most famous account of the complete abnegation of the *samurai,* which could lead them to lay down their lives for their master.

Clan warfare

The clans of the leading noble families and the warrior caste became more influential in 1156 when the emperor Sutoku, isolated and losing his grip on power, was forced to appeal to them for protection. The clan chiefs tried to take over the government but were so undermined by their rivalry and their fight for supremacy that the warriors

Above: a *samurai* warrior.

HONOUR AND SACRIFICE 69

seized the real power. In the provinces fighting continued and the power of the warriors gradually became a *fait accompli*.

Large numbers of *bushi* were recruited and maintained in the late 13th century when the Mongols, backed by the Chinese and Korean armies, tried twice to invade the island of Honshu (in 1274

Craftsmen skilled in making the various pieces of armour (below) – visors, helmets, saddles, stirrups, saddles, bows, arrows and insignia of command – enjoyed special status. Because of the

and 1281). The size of the Mongol armies prompted a change in weapons and strategies. Until then the warriors had mainly been mounted; now they had to fight on foot, using swords and halberds. Such was the carnage that the *samurai* had to alter the design of their armour.

The one-piece cuirasses that they had worn in the past were made more flexible, with metal strips fastened with leather straps and woven silk.

importance and mystical connotations of swords, armourers had pride of place. They wore white tunics like priests and carried out ritual purifications. The moment at which they quenched the blade was believed to have religious significance.

Armour through the ages

Armour (*tanko*) was designed both to protect the *samurai* and to make an impression on the enemy. From the Heian period onwards it was made of several sections covering the various parts of the body. It was light (only about 10 kilos or 22 lbs) to allow freedom of movement. As different weapons came into use (bows and arrows, swords, firearms) its function and appearance changed. Opposite and left: 16th–18th-century armour.

Iron and silk

The suit of armour had to be easy to put on quickly. Several layers of undergarments formed a kind of padding to which the straps of the armour were attached. The crude, gilded or lacquered iron strips were held in place by solid rivets or sometimes multi-coloured silk braid. The helmet and neck protector were vital, as it was customary for vanquished enemies to be beheaded. The helmet bore the clan emblem. The development of armour owes a great deal to the Myochin master armourers. Eventually the armour became so magnificent that since the 19th century it has been used only for ceremonial occasions and important collections and no longer serves any useful purpose.

Opposite left and left: two 19th-century suits of armour. Opposite centre above: an 18th-century helmet. Opposite centre below: the lower part of a mask dating from the 18th century.

The Way of the Sword and the Way of the Bow

In these battles the *samurai*, under the rules of *bushidō*, regarded their weapons as instruments that translated their mental processes into action. They tried to perfect them, decorate them and establish standards for them so that their beauty reflected their noble purpose.

In the minds of the *samurai* the sword was a sacred object, the purity of the blade symbolizing the warrior's soul. Even the withdrawal of the sword from the scabbard had significance. The long sword (*katana*) and short sword (*wakasashi*) could only be worn by the *samurai* caste. The pair of swords, known as the *daishō*, was symbolic of the dignity and power of their caste. The weapons were made up of several artistically decorated pieces. The scabbard could be in any style, from very plain natural wood to richly decorated gold lacquer embellished with a coat of arms (*mon*). The hilt (*tsuka*), guard (*tsuba*) and silk cords were also skilfully crafted.

The warriors developed a philosophy for the use of the bow, the Way of the Bow (*kyudo*). The 13th-century *samurai* used a Mongol-style bow but invented their own larger version.

The sword (below) was the physical symbol of the *samurai's* courage and loyalty. It was a religious object in an intellectual cult of honour and not simply a weapon. A *samurai* who lost his sword had lost his life and soldiers vanquished in battle went to pray at the shrine of Hachimen (the god of war), asking why their sword had lost its soul. The *tsuba* or sword guards (above) always had to match the scabbard, whether it was plain or richly decorated.

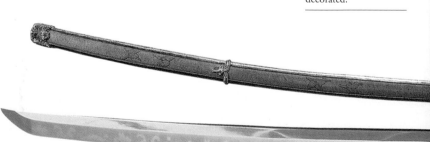

The handling of such a large bow required complete physical balance and deep concentration. The Way of the Bow is essentially a mental exercise in which man and target become one.

The austerity of the archers was in sharp contrast to the splendour of the battle armour. In time it became ceremonial armour, over which the *daimyō*, members of the leading families, wore a cloth and brocade jacket (*jimbaori*) bearing their coat of arms arranged in a heraldic code.

The biggest archery ceremonies were held in Kyōto, on the long wooden veranda of the Temple of the Thousand Buddhas, Sanjūsangen-dō (above). The firing of the bow was merely the final stage in a long process of mental preparation in which the archer purified his soul. In contemplating the target he identified with it. When the meditation had reached the point at which inside and outside merged, the arrow flew unerringly towards the centre of the target. The archer was aiming at the centre of his own being.

The battle of Sarashino

Japanese society was structured around clans comprised of the leading noble families such as the Minamoto, Taira and Ashikaga, together with their vassals, warriors and servants. The power and wealth of the families (or clans) varied widely. Sporadic fighting between the clans continued until the 16th century, when the armies of the warlords Nobunaga and Ieyasu and the Kai lord Takeda Katsuyori became involved in a bloody struggle for control of the country.

The war ended with the battle of Sarashino in 1575, in which Takeda Katsuyori's armies were annihilated. The two sides were unevenly matched. In 1549 the Jesuits had come to Japan by sea, bringing guns as an incentive to convert the country to Christianity. Nobunaga and Ieyasu accepted the deal. For the first time they used firearms on the battlefield, hidden behind wooden palisades. The Takeda clan's soldiers did not have these new weapons. Fighting on horseback in the traditional manner, they rode headlong towards the fences from which the guns were fired. There were few survivors and the Takeda clan died out completely in 1582.

This famous battle marked the beginning of radical changes in strategy, weapons and armour and, perhaps even more significantly,

Warfare changed completely with the arrival of a cargo of rifles shipped in by Jesuit missionaries from Portugal in the mid-16th century. These first ships were huge and black, with very intricate rigging. The Japanese took both a cautious and a curious attitude towards these newcomers. They studied these 'barbarians from the West' and portrayed them in paintings known as *Namban*, southern barbarians (left, a Portuguese ship). At the time Christianity was rapidly gaining ground in Japan. Shimazu Takahisa (opposite) and a number of other *daimyō* were interested in the new religion and it attracted a number of followers until it was banned in 1637.

a change of attitude. *Bushidō* remained as a code of conduct but behaviour on the battlefield now depended on efficiency rather than notions of honour.

The victors took the title *shōgun* (chief military leader) and assumed control of all affairs of state from the beginning of the 17th century, while the emperor retained a purely symbolic role.

Clan warfare ended with the bloody battle of Sekigahara in 1600 (left). The emperor conferred the title of *shōgun* on the victor, Ieyasu, chief of the Tokugawa clan. The survivors of Toyotomi's armies took refuge in the castle of Osaka and it was there that Ieyasu surrounded them and fought the last battle in 1615. He survived for only a year after that victory, which firmly established the Tokugawa clan as leaders. Ieyasu had set up the headquarters of his military government (*bafuku*) at Edo, later Tokyo, where the Tokugawa *shōguns* succeeded each other, effectively controlling the whole country while the emperors remained as figureheads in Kyōto. All government decisions were left to the all-powerful *shōgun*. In 1637 he banned Christianity in Japan. Thousands of Christian peasants rebelled and were massacred at Shimabara near Nagasaki. In 1638 the *shōgun* declared Japan closed to all westerners and ordered the execution of the sixty-one crew members of the last ship in port.

The Castle of the White Heron

The introduction of guns brought about changes in military architecture. Structures now had to be designed to withstand these weapons. In 1581 the *shōgun* Hideyoshi had a castle built at Himeji, southwest of Kyōto. It was named Shirasagijō, the Castle of the White Heron, because its graceful and elegant stepped roofs, surmounting white walls, drew the eye upwards and gave the building an appearance of lightness. The whole structure was protected by huge foundations made of large blocks of stone and by moats.

Himeji was a nerve centre that allowed the country to be kept under control from the west to the imperial capital, Kyōto. Hideyoshi, later ruler of Japan, had a fortress built there (above).

The lord's quarters were surrounded by a maze of fortified passageways, keeps, storehouses and so on, on five levels. To make the rooms less oppressive, the living quarters were decorated with magnificent brightly coloured paintings on a gold background.

The decor was designed by the painter Kanō Eitoku, son of Kanō Shoei. At the age of twenty-three Eitoku already enjoyed a considerable reputation. His youth and skill gave him the courage to work with unpainted pure gold surfaces embellished only with a few trees, rocks and birds, blending painted and unpainted areas and creating a dynamic imbalance that made the vast room very interesting. His work represents the best example of castle decor, symbolizing the power of the *shōgun*.

It took nine years to design all the internal defence systems and build the fortified Castle of the White Heron (below), which no one dared besiege. The roads leading to it were steep and bristling with traps. Eleven massive doors guarded the paths leading to the keep. A series of fortified positions behind right-angled blind curves enabled the defenders to fire unexpectedly on attackers. In the vast rooms, openings to the exterior were designed as loopholes and there were numerous trap doors in the floor. The castle was guarded by three thousand *samurai*. However, at the same time it was a place of entertainment, music and poetry befitting a *shōgun's* court (above, a screen combining lightness of composition and brilliant colours).

Zen is a school of behaviour and thought based on austerity and an appreciation of the simplest acts in life. It spread to Japan from China in the first half of the 13th century and was developed in the monasteries and on the road through itinerant monks and poets. It inspired various forms of art, including the tea ceremony, garden design and calligraphy.

CHAPTER 5

THE WAY OF ZEN

The subjects in Zen art have to be deciphered as symbols. In this painting by Hokusai (right), the Japanese Sisyphus, Hotei, is moving an object larger than himself by sheer willpower. Yūshō's old Taoist sage (opposite) is riding on a buffalo that he has finally managed to tame.

The foundations of Zen

Zen was introduced into China in the 6th century by Bodhidharma (Daruma), the first Zen patriarch. It preached paradox, contradiction, questions without answers and apparent inconsistency as ways to Enlightenment. Later on it spread to Japan through the monks of the Sōtō and Rinzai schools.

Zen differs from other traditional schools of Buddhism in that it leads to Enlightenment (*satori*) through concentration on the most trivial everyday actions. Any manual or intellectual work that brings a person out of his state of passivity is part of the process of Enlightenment. It is for this reason that Zen monks sweep the courtyards of monasteries and devote themselves to the most humble tasks.

In particular, any creation or art form that expresses the inner self is a lesson or at least a testimony to others. Work of this kind plays on the notion of time. Life must be captured instantly and not altered by any digressions of style. Some part always has to be left unfinished or empty so that the spectator can complete the movement himself or herself, be free to perceive the forms and understand the symbolism. In the Zen concept of Enlightenment a work of art only has validity through the life it conveys. It is always incomplete, open like the circle of infinity, barely legible like the final dry strokes of calligraphy, sketched with a humour that turns monks and gods into evanescent outlines.

The art of ink drawing

Most Zen artists such as Sesson and Sōami (in the

In the position known as *zazen* (below) the spine is straight, the chin tucked in as if the head was holding up the sky. This is the proper state for body and mind: not looking for anything, not waiting for anything, simply being there, here and now. The outer and inner world are both infinite; the gaze is like an opening door. There is no world, no 'I', nothing but an objective consciousness. The position of the hands is also part of this movement of energy between the outer and the inner world (below, the monk Tokiyori).

The mythical figure Jitoku, personifying innocence, endlessly swept the sand on the monastery paths. In Zen tradition he represents one of the ways to knowledge. Tawayara Sōtatsu painted this very simple portrait of him in ink in the 17th century (above).

Daruma (left), shown here in red Indian-style clothes, brought Zen to Japan. His gaze reflects his power. The function of these paintings was to help the faithful escape spiritual torpor, ignorance and illusion.

In this painting (left) by Sesson Shūkei (1504–89), the different intensities of black are used as colour values and the non-coloured background represents the infinity of space. It symbolizes the whole cosmos in which there is no void. Our minds have to restore the link between every part of the world existing beyond what is visible.

Muromachi period) and the most celebrated of all, Sesshū, were considered to be on a par with monks. Sesshū went to China in the late 15th century to perfect his technique. On returning to Japan he set up a studio and taught ink drawing to the leading artists of his time. He himself specialized in painting landscapes with steep mountains and gnarled dry trees, inspired by Song art. In the 17th century the painter Fūgai drew mythical Zen figures like the founder, Daruma, and the monk Hotei.

Zen-inspired pictures are drawn in Chinese ink, diluted (*sumi-e*) to varying degrees to produce shades ranging from the deepest black to smoky grey. The world they depict is real but not realistic; it has shapes, but they are constantly changing. The free and austere style of these works encourages liberation of the spirit.

The art of calligraphy (*shō*) was much admired by the warrior caste. The demands and mental and physical disciplines it imposed on its practitioners had a great deal in common with their own code of ethics. They saw a similarity between the rapid and assured movements used in calligraphy and their own striving for inner perfection, the first rule of *bushidō*.

The character *Ryu* (above), drawn by an eighty-three-year-old calligrapher in the 18th century with a single stroke of the pen, means dragon. It coils back on itself and finishes in a single dry stroke. The two dots look like the animal's eyes. This art lies between symbolism and representation.

The superimposed ideograms in this calligraphy (left), signed by the monk Nichiren (1222–82), evoke a repetition of the *sutra*. The calm order of the characters drawn by Daisui Zengi in the 18th century (above) calls to mind 'a peaceful hut in the mountains, in the midst of nature'.

雪
舟

Sesshū Tōyō (1420–1506), son of a *samurai* from the Oda family in Bitchū province, was the main pioneer of Zen painting or *suibokuga* (ink painting) in Japan. At the age of twelve he was enrolled as a novice in the nearby monastery of Shōkoku-ji. In 1467 he went to China, where he studied Zen, travelled and learned Song painting. Landscapes with steep mountains and gnarled pines made a deep impression on him and he achieved a synthesis of Chinese and Japanese painting. His technique of angular strokes and pointillism gives his tortured compositions great power. Adapting paintings by Chinese scholars, he created a characteristically Japanese style that inspired many artists, including Sōami Motonobu (1476–1559).

The tea ceremony

The tea ceremony (*chanoyū*) was introduced into Japan from China at the beginning of the 13th century by Eisai (1141–1215), founder of the Rinzai school of Zen. The gestures and procedure form part of a ritual whose rules are laid down in *The Book of Tea* (*chajing*). At the end of the 15th century the *shōgun* Ashikaga Yoshimasa had a pavilion built for the tea ceremony at his villa in Kyōto, where the tea master Murata Juko officiated specially for him and

Above and opposite: the tea master takes water from the kettle (*kama*) with a long wooden spoon (*hishaku*). The bowl (*chawan*) is placed opposite him and on the left is the *chaïre* containing the special powdered green tea for the tea ceremony, the *chanoyū*.

his guests. Through the famous master Senno Rikyū (1521–91), the *chanoyū* spread to all levels of cultured society in the 16th century and the 'Way of Tea' (*sadō*) was established. The aesthetic principles followed the Zen ideal of simplicity (*wabi* – simplicity, *sabi* – wear showing the passing of time).

The measurements of the room in which the ceremony was held were now subject to very strict rules. It had to be four *tatami* mats or about nine square metres (96 square feet) in area. The room was entered through a low door. Inside, the muted colours harmonized with the green of the tea and the materials (wood and paper) were evocative of nature. It was important to display an ink painting or piece of calligraphy in harmony with the spirit of the tea and an *ikebana* (flower arrangement) in as pure and simple a style as possible in a *tokonoma* (meditation area). The objects used for the ceremony were made of natural materials such as iron, earth and bamboo. Although rough in appearance, they were in fact very skilfully made. The *chawan* (ceramic bowls) came from the Bizen, Seto, Shino, Raku and Oribe kilns.

The bowls used for the tea ceremony (above) were made in kilns in the Kensai region. They were in varying shapes, flat or tall, and the colours of the glaze differed, white for the *shino*, orangey-red for the *raku*. Black was also a popular colour. The colour had to harmonize with the green of the tea and the bowls had to be simple in design and fit the hand gestures.

The art of the Zen garden

The tea house was usually in a slightly secluded position, in a small garden set aside for meditation, and was designed entirely on *chanoyū* principles. Flowering plants were rare and the trees were chosen for their dark foliage, to create an atmosphere of harmony, respect, purity and tranquillity (*wa, kei, sei, jaku*) and to give a natural impression. Some features, such as the irregular stones in a path of multi-coloured shingle, the bamboo, the stone lantern and the bowl with a long-handled bamboo spoon resting on it for purification, were found in every garden.

One of the earliest gardens, the Koketera or 'moss garden', was designed by Mūso Soseki at the beginning of the 14th century. It contained a lake and islands symbolizing the Buddha's paradise. The mosses in various shades of green created a calm atmosphere encouraging contemplation. Soseki also designed the Tenryu-ji garden, consisting mainly of stones and bushes that had been trimmed and arranged according to their flowering season. Zen temple gardens were often designed by painters. At the end of the 15th century, for instance, Sesshū drew up the plans for the Tōfuku-ji temple, in the style of Chinese paintings.

The Golden Pavilion (Kinkaku-ji) was part of the residence of the *shōgun* Yoshimitsu in the 15th century, known at the time as *Kitayama-dono* (the palace of the northern mountains). The whole complex was converted into a monastery, of which only the Kinkaku-ji remains (below). It is on three floors. The extraordinary beauty of the Kinkaku-ji comes from its design, based on very precise calculations.

At the Silver Pavilion (Ginkaku-ji) built in the mid-16th century, the lake was bordered on one side by an undulating river of sand with a symbolic arrangement of stones based on the late 12th-century *Secret Book of Gardens* (*Sakutei-ki*). In front of the pavilion was a large area of raked white sand raised into a mound, designed to be viewed by

moonlight to evoke the unreal whiteness of the sea and mountains.

The famous Golden Pavilion (Kinkaku-ji) built by the *shōgun* Yoshimitsu in 1397 is magically reflected in the calm waters of a lake. Along with the Katsura villa, it is one of the most impressive architectural and garden complexes in Japan.

'Dry' gardens

'Dry' or sand and stone gardens gave monks an empty space for their meditations, the movements deep down betrayed only by undulations on the surface of the sand. At Daitoku-ji natural and highly symbolic irregular stones represented the silhouette of the meditating Buddha, at Daisen-in the Buddhist trinity and the complexity of the universe carefully arranged as a microcosm. However, the most remarkable feature at the Daisen-in monastery,

Those entering a monastery garden have to purify themselves beforehand with cool water flowing from a bamboo (opposite). A long-handled spoon is used for the ritual ablutions.

The monastery buildings are surrounded by a series of gardens similar in style to the adjoining rooms. A temple might have a 'dry garden' for meditation and a 'moss garden' (above) or water garden edged with trees with foliage that is in harmony with the rest.

The term 'dry garden', as compared with a garden with trees, is used only for monastery gardens. The dry garden is an empty area of white sand conducive to contemplation and an inner vacuum, creating a sense of balance in those who manage to enter this abstract world with their eyes open. The most important gardens are in Kyōto, including those at the Ryōan-ji (opposite bottom), Daitoku-ji (left), Nansen-ji, Daisen in (opposite top) and Ryogen-in. The sand is raked by monks every day so that the regular furrows form a sort of calm ocean and cannot be disturbed by anything, not even the wind. Three mounds of sand, arranged so that only two are ever visible at any one time, or fifteen stones that cannot all be seen at the same time, are a sign to those who observe that the world cannot be perceived in its entirety. Anything that is invisible to them they must find within themselves. The symbolically arranged raised stones are positioned at a ritual attended only by monks.

designed by the painter Sōami in 1513, is undoubtedly the rectangular expanse of white sand, raked every day into three mounds. Whichever vantage point these are viewed from, one is always invisible. The aim is to create an intense feeling of reverence.

The sand garden at Daisen-in and the garden at Ryōan-ji, probably the most famous of the Zen monastery gardens, have certain features in common. The expanse of white sand is regularly raked into waves around fifteen stones in irregular shapes and sizes, arranged in a perceptible but not obvious order. The Ryōan-ji has links with Shintō and each sacred stone has to be positioned according to type. This is a clear and pure space, made for the gods. The impression of an area set aside for the invisible –

Matsuo Bashō (1644–94) was a poet. In his *haiku* (short poems) similar in style to *koan*, or Zen parables, he pretends to 'let the words muse on the words' (above). Like Sengai, Hakuin, a monk and leading Zen reformer, used ink painting and poetic form in his teachings in the 18th century. The 18th-century poet Hitomaro (opposite) belonged to the *Rokkasen* group of poets, and produced very elegant verse.

meditation and the gods – is reinforced by the dense vegetation that has grown up outside the walls of the sand and stone garden at the Ryōan-ji monastery. Like ink drawings and poems, the gardens are a medium for Zen, the dry road to Enlightenment.

Monks and poets

Poetry in Japan springs from the meeting of cultivated minds and it is one of the foundations of the calligrapher's art. *Koan* (problems that admit no apparent logical solution) are a succinct and symbolic expression of Zen thought. They are deliberately provocative, a way of making people think.

They have similarities with poetry, notably the *haiku*, a short and allusive poem developed in the second half of the 17th century by Bashō, whose very name conjures up this verse form, and later by Issa. Literature, painting and later printmaking were to a large extent inspired by the world of poetry.

When the Edo period began in 1615 under the Tokugawa *shōgun*, poetry was a natural link between the new *ukiyo-e* culture dedicated to a secular belief in the ephemeral world and the rigid code of Zen, encouraging self-awareness in the present. The gradations of the ink and the marks of the brush in calligraphy were suggestive of both eternity and time passing.

At the end of the 17th century people from the lowest level of society, unconnected with the temples or court and without any civic rights, took over Edo, the *shōgun's* city. They achieved this feat solely through their talent and their genius in inventing a completely new artistic idiom, *ukiyo-e*, the art of the floating world. Prints and *Kabuki* theatre were its main forms of expression.

CHAPTER 6

THE EDO PERIOD: LIFE AS THEATRE

The master print-maker Kitagawa Utamaro (1754–1806; left, *Two Women Stirring up the Fire*) and Tsuchida Soetsu (1660–1745), who made the medicine box (*inro*) on the right, enhanced the reputations of their patrons, the townspeople or *chonin*, by creating beautiful objects for their everyday use.

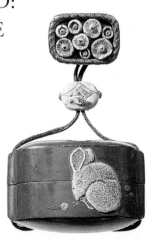

A new social class

After the Portuguese ships arrived in the 17th century, some Japanese merchants amassed such huge fortunes that they became bankers to the nobility and the *samurai*. The titles and residences they bought made them the equals of the most powerful figures in society, but they still had no political or social rights. Finding themselves excluded from feudal circles, they created a different kind of community, a 'republic' of artists in which talent was a substitute for nobility and freedom.

Entrances to stalls were screened by *noren* (left), patterned cloth curtains also used for advertising. The most famous had a distinctive sign like a coat of arms.

The rich merchants acted as patrons, commissioning new works of art with subjects drawn from the everyday life of the *chonin* (townspeople), the new *Kabuki* theatre and the courtesans celebrated for their beauty, music and dancing. Painters, writers, publishers and a cultivated elite gathered around them and intellectual activity and taste flourished.

The streets of Edo and Osaka (above) were a meeting place for all kinds of people: monks, warriors, pedlars, working-class women, courtesans and their servants, actors and their admirers.

The early 17th century: a turning point

At the beginning of the Edo period in 1615, the *shōguns* of the Tokugawa clan set up their government and court in the new capital, Edo (later Tokyo). This era represented a turning point in art, from which the general principles of *ukiyo-e* evolved. The new art form retained links with ancient traditions.

While the artists of the Kanō and Tosa schools continued to design sumptuous palaces for the *daimyō*, painters like Matabei illustrated the pleasures of a society of aesthetes in genre paintings, including the famous *Dancers*, street scenes or garden festivals. These secular themes were a new source of inspiration, a radical departure from the literary, religious and aristocratic subject matter of previous works.

The Portuguese in Japan played a part in these cultural

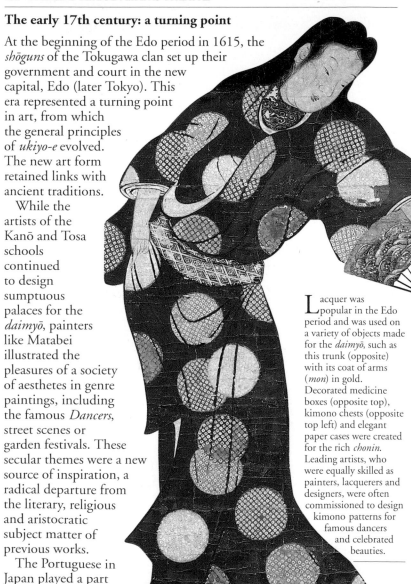

Lacquer was popular in the Edo period and was used on a variety of objects made for the *daimyō*, such as this trunk (opposite) with its coat of arms (*mon*) in gold. Decorated medicine boxes (opposite top), kimono chests (opposite top left) and elegant paper cases were created for the rich *chonin*. Leading artists, who were equally skilled as painters, lacquerers and designers, were often commissioned to design kimono patterns for famous dancers and celebrated beauties.

changes, trading with merchants in the port of Nagasaki who shipped in their new and exotic foods and distributed them all over the country. This trade encouraged the creation of decorated objects, which the designers Kōrin and Kenzan turned into a major art form. In the Edo period elegant everyday objects such as *netsuke* (ivory or wood buttons), *inro* (medicine boxes divided into compartments, worn on the belt), pipe cases, lacquer combs, gold and mother-of-pearl encrusted chests were much sought after by connoisseurs and later by collectors.

•Genre painting• preceded the introduction of printmaking, but the two had a number of features in common. *Dancers* (detail opposite) by Iwasa Matabei (c. 1578–1650) is a fine example of an art form that is dying out. The red, black and white bring out the magnificence of the clothes, recalling the splendour of the *shōgun's* court. The dancers were the precursors of the first *Kabuki* theatre, their gracefulness inspiring the *onnagata* actors who played the female roles. Two hundred years later their fluid movements inspired the Nabis when Japanese art became an influence in Europe during the 19th century. The portrait of Madame Monet with a fan was based on Matabei's painting.

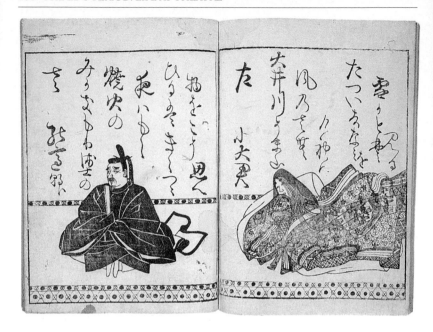

Ukiyo-e

Ukiyo-e is the art of the printmakers and the painters and writers who worked in the same style. The word, coined by the writer Asai Ryōi in 1661, means 'pictures of the floating world'. It embraces the Buddhist idea of the transience of the visible world and its poetic melancholy. Conscious of the passing of time and passionately devoted to the simple things in life, artists began to draw on their own lives for inspiration, which was completely unprecedented.

The relationship between painters, writers and poets was the same for all *ukiyo-e*. The early printed works, regarded as the first examples of this art form, were books or albums based on romances and old tales or the works of the thirty-six classical poets. The famous *Sanju rokkasen* (*The Thirty-six Poets*), published in 1610, with calligraphy attributed to Kōetsu, is illustrated with prints of the poets.

Printmaking developed at the beginning of the 17th century. The technique makes great demands on the printmaker's skills. All the lines (often as fine as a hair) or the flat tints indicated by the artist are carved on a block of cherry wood. At the end the printer attaches the paper carefully to the ink- or paint-coated plates while it is still wet, using just a few reference marks.

The first print to be made (above) was a black-and-white album, *Sanju rokkasen* (*The Thirty-six Poets*) in 1610.

Buddhist monks were the first to use wood engraving in the Chinese style for pictures and religious texts. The monks set up schools for the children of the *chonin* and taught them to read and write, introducing them in this way to Japan's traditional culture. Without this teaching a whole section of the population would have been excluded from the culture accessible only to children of the nobility and the warrior caste. It was the dominance of the large monastic orders that made this radical departure possible. The *ukiyo-e* artists who had attended their schools were familiar with not only the major Buddhist texts but also the work of the famous poets and the *Genji monogatari*.

The portraits of poets are attributed to Tosa Mitsushige; the calligraphy is by Kōetsu. They were printed separately, using movable characters. *Soga monogatari (The Drama of the Soga Brothers,* c. 1646; above) was coloured by hand in saffron and then moss green. The additional colours put the print aesthetically on a par with painting. Left: a print of an agricultural festival (*matsuri*) by Jihei, coloured in green and yellow.

Master printmakers

The first prints were simple, printed just in black and white (*sumizuri-e*). The first artist to become prominent in this field was Moronobu, regarded as a master because of his confident strokes and lifelike compositions. As well as producing a large number of individual prints, he illustrated many famous texts such as the *Genji monogatari* (1680) and *Earth and Wood Pictures* (1683), which had already been highlighted by hand with ochre and yellow mineral colouring. These early embellishments, appealing to the taste of a public accustomed to shimmering colours because of painting and screens, inspired artists to look for ways of printing in different colours.

Nevertheless, many artists continued to produce black-and-white prints. Sukenobu (18th century) specialized in scenes from the

The first two-colour print, *benizuri-e* (below), was by Masanobu (1750).

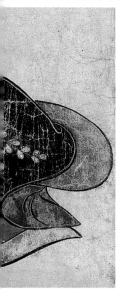

Morals in the hedonistic *ukiyo-e* society were liberal enough for 'educational' scenes (*shunga* or 'pictures of spring') to be published in books such as *Notes on the Lives of a Hundred Women* (1723) by Sukenobu, who also drew erotic scenes (opposite). The colours are so brilliant that the print is like a painting. The eroticism comes from the strength and harmony of the colours more than the actual subject matter, a couple lying under a kimono.

everyday life of women and erotic subjects (*shunga*). Sugimira Jihei (c. 1690) was the first to depict courtesans and actors in a bold and simple style. He was a precursor of the Kaigetsudō group – named after the painter (1671–1743) – who were noted for their portraits of women and for large prints similar to paintings. In the same period Kiyomasu, founder of the Torii tradition, specialized in pictures of *Kabuki* theatre and actors in their most famous roles.

Between 1745 and 1750 colour prints became more common. Toyonobu and Masanobu succeeded in printing pink and green (*benizuri-e*), a major advance in printmaking. In the same period Masanobu added yellow, brown and ochre with the *urushi-e* technique. However, it was not until *kentō*, a 'trick of the trade', began to be used systematically by the publisher Uemura Kichiemeon that all the colours were printed together. Placed at the corner of the plates, it acted as a stop for the sheet of paper, which was transferred with great accuracy from wood

A significant change occurred in the development of printmaking in the 1760s when Harunobu (1724–70) took full advantage of the opportunities provided by *kentō* to create the wonderful *nishiki-e* (brocade prints). Harunobu was also the only artist known to incorporate sun and shadow in a print. A young woman sheltering under a parasol is looking at her shadow on the ground (above). Japanese art does not usually reflect changing light and the passage of time; the use of shadow is unusual.

The large *Kabuki* theatre opened in Edo in the late 18th century was extremely popular and has remained so ever since. *Kabuki* was established in its definitive form in the 1660s. In the body of the theatre were rows of seats and the leading actor came on stage via a long aisle (*hanamichi*) running through the audience. The very complex stage sets allowed changes of scenery for the performance of plays based on legends and epic tales and the world of the imagination. The heroes – the leading actor (*tachiyaki*), his enemy (*katakiyaku*) and the rest of the cast – are stock characters. The works of the famous writer Chikamatsu Monzaemon included *The Forty-seven Rōnin*.

to wood so that the different colours could be added successively. The process was first used by Harunobu between 1760 and 1768. The colours he obtained were so subtle and harmonious that his works were known as 'brocade prints' (*nishiki-e*). He also revolutionized the subject matter of prints, drawing his inspiration from routine actions in the everyday life of women and children, rediscovering the wonder of the old masters in the simple beauty of lives that had been completely ignored by the official artists.

Kabuki

In the late 16th century a new theatrical genre developed, based on dance and puppet shows. The themes of the plays are derived from epics and legends. *Kabuki* soon became popular and dramatists like Chikamatsu Monzaemon wrote plays for the leading dynasties of actors, identifiable by their coats of arms (*mon*) and stage make-up. In 1629 the *shōgun*, determined to stamp out immorality in the theatre, decreed that all parts should be played by men.

This new theatrical genre, with its stage, spectators, boxes and legendary heroes, was an endless source of

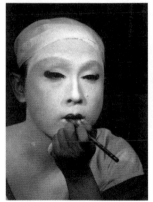

Under an edict issued in 1629 women were banned from the stage and replaced by young men. In 1649 a further edict was issued and from then on all female roles (*onnagata*) were taken by older men. The actor redraws his eyes, eyebrows and mouth on a foundation of very thick white make-up. He is then dressed in his female costume and finally he puts on the wig. Sharaku was merciless in his portrayals of these heroes: the actor Matsumoto Yonesaburo (below) in the *onnagata* role of Kenaizaka No Shosho (c. 1794).

inspiration for the *ukiyo-e* artists. Toyokuni (1769–1825) and Shunshō (1726–92) were among the leading printmakers who followed the actors both in the theatre and around town. The most famous was undoubtedly Toshusai Sharaku, who produced all his work within the space of one year (1794). This marvellous artist, probably an actor himself, painted nothing but close-up portraits of actors, so realistic that he was suspected of stealing their souls. He was murdered.

Each role in the *Kabuki* repertoire was allocated to a family of actors, who played it from generation to generation. Like the noble families, every family had a coat of arms that identified a particular actor. The most celebrated dynasty was (and still is) the Danjurō family, who wear large red kimonos patterned with three white squares. They play the hero who rights wrongs and is applauded every time he appears (centre, Kiyoshige's portrait of the actor Danjurō in stage costume). In the streets of Edo famous actors had star status, rivalled only by the leading courtesans. Printmakers were eager to draw their portraits, over which their many fans immediately fought. Left: Danjurō V playing Saka Kintoki by Shunshō (c. 1781). Opposite: the actor Segawa Kikunojo in an *onnagata* role wearing the Sai-on-ji coat of arms, by Shunchō, Shunshō's pupil (c. 1770).

The Yoshiwara district in Edo and the Shimabara district in Kyōto were full of music, laughter and conversation. The artists found a spirit of rivalry amongst the courtesans bought and educated by the tea-house owners (left, a tea house in Kyōto, by Shigenaga, c. 1745). Some spent virtually all their time there, their liberal and revolutionary ideas arousing the suspicions of the authorities. For them caricature was a form of freedom of expression and it was tolerated (below, *Kabuki* actors by Kuniyoshi) as long as it was not aimed at the *shōgun* or his entourage.

The Yoshiwara district

Another major source of inspiration for *ukiyo-e* and certainly the most famous was the world of the Yoshiwara, 'green houses', named after the area of marshes and bamboos on the other side of the river Sumida in Edo, which was a centre for entertainment, beauty and intellectual life. In this 'red light' district lived the leading courtesans (*oiran*), their young followers (*maiko*) and later the *geishas*, or hostesses. Famous actors and painters, writers and publishers, including the great Tsutaya, the leading printmaker of his day, flocked to the district. The artists' colony that they established was a hotbed of competition and rivalry, the new ideas that it generated so disturbing to the authorities that the district was kept under surveillance by soldiers and censors. Prints and books were scrutinized and any subversive material banned. The penalties were severe. Tsutaya's shop was completely destroyed when he disobeyed an edict and made fun of an official in a satirical

drawing. Utamaro had to wear wooden handcuffs for fifty days, making it impossible for him to work.

Even the landscape painters represented a threat to the authorities, simply because they had a sense of humour. Hokusai had an irreverent attitude to officialdom and scorned honours. Hiroshige sketched caricatures on the street and preferred the company of monks to the court. Kuniyoshi drew an unflattering portrait of the *shōgun's* favourite.

The name Utamaro appears on the fan in this *shunga* print (c. 1788, probably the first of an erotic series), one of the most famous examples of *ukiyo-e* art. The lovers' faces are lost in an embrace and we are outsiders (or voyeurs). The eroticism comes from the subtle

Although all these artists in the Edo period specialized mainly in prints, they did not neglect the other aspect of *ukiyo-e* art, painting. They were familiar with the painters of the Tosa and Kanō schools and had often worked with them, training with them in the same traditional techniques. Moronobu, for instance, painted a pair of screens depicting the lives of actors in the wings of the *Kabuki* theatre, the Nakamuraza in Edo, in pure Tosa style.

details rather than the actual subject matter. Kitagawa Utamaro (1754–1806) made Yoshiwara his workplace, living with his models and becoming their lover or confidant. He was never short of female subjects wanting to be immortalized.

Western influence

In the 18th century a few artists and scholars travelled to Nagasaki, opposite the Dutch colony on the island of Deshima. It was the only European settlement permitted by the shogunate authorities after Japan was closed to foreigners in 1638. The Dutch acted as a sort of embassy for western culture, introducing the Japanese to the works of the Polish astronomer Copernicus, the French surgeon Ambroise Paré and the French painter and inventor of the daguerreotype, Louis-Jacques-Mandé Daguerre. The prints of Italian paintings inspired a curiosity about western perspective that revolutionized the Japanese view of the world and

After Japan was closed to foreigners, a Dutch colony survived in Deshima and the Japanese went there to study the language and writing of the 'barbarians' (above, a double-sided book).

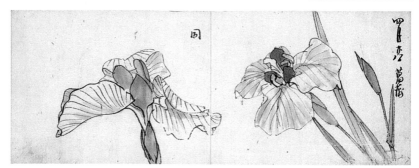

especially landscapes, inherited from Taoist philosophy.

The Dutch also introduced the Japanese to such subjects as botany and anatomy. Western books played a crucial role in the development of Japanese art and the dissemination of knowledge.

In the 18th century societies commissioned painters and poets to produce *surimono* (square) prints on the theme of books, reading and writing.

The Japanese and the Dutch shared a passion for plants, exchanging bulbs and grafts and trying to adapt them to different climates. Irises, grown in the Japanese 'water gardens', were the inspiration for many artists (above, Nanzan, 19th century).

阿蘭陀フラスカ之藍之圖

U tagawa Toyoharu (1735–1814) modelled his prints (left) on Dutch engravings of Italian paintings of Venice and the ruins in Rome. For the first time western concepts of perspective and space were used in Japanese art. Objects from the West, such as glass and porcelain, which were considered rare and exotic (below), also found their way into Japanese pictures.

The *surimono* were mainly still life, combining graphic art and design. Leading artists such as

116

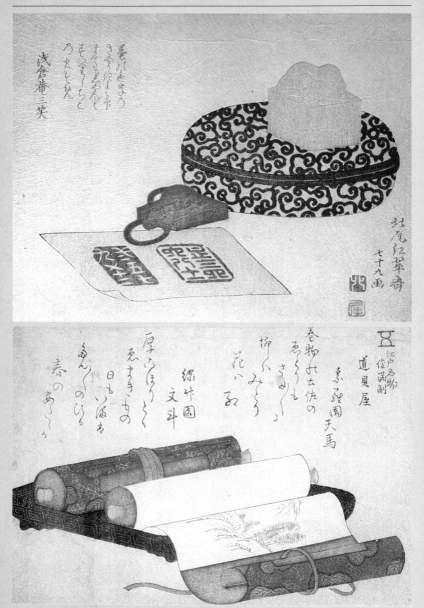

玉の名み
もろきろ〜てらら
孫寿亭子
こしの花を
さくられて
久島

花栖亭 真芳

狂歌堂

Societies commissioned *surimono* from poets and painters, who created a joint work for a special event or a New Year's greeting. The play of light brought out the full subtlety of the silver and gold highlights and white on white embossing on thick, square, fluffy paper. Still life is one of the most sophisticated themes of the *surimono*, conveying both the reality and the poetry of everyday life. Opposite above: *Seals* by Shigenaga (1739–1820). Opposite below: *Emaki Painting Scrolls* by Shunman (1757–1820). Left: *Bookcase* by Gakutei (1786–1868). Below: *Koto* (a musical instrument) by Shinsai (1764–1820).

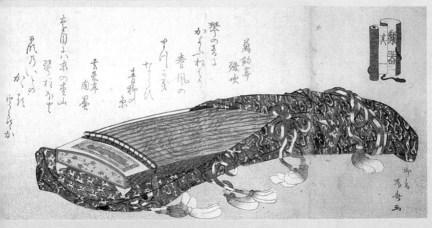

Shunman, Eishi, Gakutei and Hokusai worked in this style and developed it into a sophisticated art form.

Three eccentrics

Two new schools of painting developed alongside printmaking: the Nanga or Bunjinga school, a return to the Chinese model of academic painting, and the Shijo school, based on a naturalistic observation of the plant and animal world.

Jakūchū, Shohaku and Rōsetsu, three artists living on the margins of society, were branded 'eccentrics' because the work they produced in Kyōto did not conform to any of the rules. For them artistic creation was a way of expressing freedom, breaking away from the grip of orthodox religion and the all-pervasive state control. The simplicity and apparent inconsistencies of Zen united them in their desire to escape formalism.

Itō Jakūchū (1716–1800) drew cockerels – red fighting cocks and the black cockerels that crowed at dawn – as a daily exercise in meditation. Soga Shohaku (1730–81) made fun of officialdom with his screens depicting respectable figures looking slightly inebriated and mad on a gold background next to an old pine tree in the Kanō style, painted with a brush soaked in ink. Around 1785 Nagasawa Rōetsu accepted a huge commission for 180 sliding panels for temples in Kii province. He painted elephants, buffaloes playing with fat puppies and young ravens, parodying the naturalistic Shijo school. A multi-talented virtuoso, he transformed animals and plants into kindly monsters and strange vegetables, playing with

Shohaku was eccentric and revolutionary, mocking the authorities and flouting tradition. He threw the ink on to the paper as if in a fit of rage, showing revered figures in a state of inebriation. Above: the Heian poet Ono no Komachi, well known for her beauty and elegance, has become a shaggy-haired old woman with a crazed expression.

In 1738 Jakūchū, whose name means 'like the void', became the disciple of a Zen monk in Kyōto. Later he developed an interest in botany and zoology and for some time drew chickens and cockerels in a pure classical style (left). He gradually developed a very Chinese style, but used it to illustrate episodes from the life of the Buddha in the form of vegetables. Rōsetsu is reputed to have shown signs of eccentricity. He was particularly fond of painting life-size elephants on screens or sliding doors in temples and palaces (above).

In 1831 Katsushika Hokusai produced a series of eight prints of waterfalls to which pilgrims travel to worship the forces of nature (*kami*). The print of the Amida waterfall (left) is famous for its composition, both realistic and symbolic, the gushing waterfall contrasting with the sinuous lines of the crater from which it emerges. Three travellers are picnicking peacefully in this rugged landscape of rocks and water. *A Wave at Kanagawa* (pp. 124–5) in the *Thirty-six Views of Mount Fuji* series is impressive for the breadth of its composition and its accurate observation of the foam on a wave as it curls back on itself. The picture is now recognized as a great work of art.

perspective and reversing large and small so that the naturalistic became fantastic.

Images of nature: Hokusai, Hiroshige, Kuniyoshi

Ukiyo-e was an extraordinary window on the world, linking every form of cultural expression. Artists working in Edo, Kyōto and Osaka were in regular contact and influenced each other. They travelled along the ancient Tokaido road (between Edo and Kyōto) or went into the countryside, where rich and

Although Kuniyoshi was more at home with ghosts, legends and his fantastic universe, he also drew this very simple composition (opposite top) of a landscape in a snowstorm, with the monk Nichiren toiling painfully up the hill. The print is part of the *Koso Goichidai Ryakuzu* series, dating from 1855.

The ninety-first print in the *Hundred Views of Edo* (c. 1857) by Andō Hiroshige (below) shows the river at the Akiba shrine. In an autumnal landscape two travellers have come to look at the maple trees (*momiji*), a ritual that has its spring counterpart in the cherry tree festival (*sakura*). In those two seasons the Japanese take to the roads and their worship of nature turns them into poets and painters, sensitive to the transient beauty of life. Hiroshige made engravings of the main stages on the Tokaido road. In the view of Hakone (overleaf), he created a composition on several planes that foreshadows modern art.

cultured farmers gave them a sympathetic reception and showed a lively interest in their work. In an inward-looking country people travelled as much as possible, visiting the well-known temples, the homes of the old poets and famous natural sights such as the Nachi waterfall, Lake Biwa and the Ise rocks. In the 19th century Japan was a closed world and the Japanese, like all island peoples, dreamed of escape.

Hokusai, Hiroshige and Kuniyoshi, three contemporaries, went to visit Dogen, Genai and Shiba Kokan, who were studying 'western sciences' with the Dutch in Nagasaki near the island of Deshima. The ideas of perspective they brought back with them had a profound influence on their work.

The whole of nature became their studio. Hiroshige (1797–1858) illustrated the *Fifty-three Stages of the Tokaido*, *Views of the Provinces* and the *Hundred Views of Edo*. Hokusai (1760–1849) went to the foot of the great waterfalls and observed Mount Fuji in all weathers and in different lights.

He put together thousands of sketches reflecting his insatiable curiosity about plants, animals, bridges, wrestlers, tightrope walkers, children's games and hundreds of other scenes in the fifteen-volume *Mangwa*, a sort of living encyclopedia full of nostalgia for a world that would never be the same again after this 'old man obsessed with painting'.

Kuniyoshi (1797–1861) lived with his fifty-three cats. Just as they could see in the dark, he saw through time. Perhaps they were looking at the same scenes: ancient battles, immortal heroes, ghosts still roaming the world, monsters in the raging grey and white seas

In his *Mangwa* (below) Hokusai strives to understand every aspect of Japan as it came to the end of an era.

and a monk all alone in a boundless space. Kuniyoshi was no stranger to fear. He conjured up warriors, legendary monks and monsters from the depths of Japan's mythical past.

Encounters with the West

Craftsmanship, like art, flourished as people travelled around the country, contributing to the vitality and revival of Japan's varied cultures. The arrival of Commodore Perry's American 'black ships' in 1853 was not the same as a western invasion. The opening up of the ports gave the Japanese access to the modern world and its technology: trains, trams and steam engines. After discovering the sewing machine, they gave up the kimono for everyday wear and started wearing 'stitched' clothes. However, the most important innovation was without doubt the advent of the first newspapers and caricatures, destroying all taboos on information and the way in which officials were represented. Humour was no longer censored. Photography in particular brought about enormous changes. The instantaneous results satisfied the traditional obsession for seizing a piece of the ephemeral and changing world. Later on the cinema became the real contemporary art of Japan.

View on a Fine Breezy Day (opposite) in the *Thirty-six Views of Mount Fuji* series is one of Hokusai's most famous prints. Van Gogh 'copied' several of Hiroshige's works, including *Rain Shower on Ohashi Bridge* (overleaf).

The early European photographers soon attracted Japanese followers, who often chose as their subject matter the scenes depicted in the prints, showing Japan as it really was.

DOCUMENTS

"In this world we walk on the roof of hell and look at the flowers."

Issa (1763–1827), *Shadowless Ants*

The Secret Book of Gardens

To cultured Japanese people the early gardens were reminiscent of famous landscapes in China. The rocks hollowed out by water and the gnarled trees on mountain peaks were familiar to the well-read. Over the years a very precise system of symbols was evolved for the design of palace and monastery gardens and various works were written on the subject. Gardens were carefully laid out to propitiate the kami, *encourage poetic contemplation or assist meditation. The* Sakutei-ki *(also known as the* Zen sai hisho, *'summary of the secrets of garden design') is one of the oldest texts, dating from the 12th century.*

'When you position the stones you must take account of the topographical features of the garden and the view of the pond'

You must also express the *fuzei* which might be evocative of a natural site whilst still retaining the original appearance of the stones.

You must remember the country's famous landscapes and bear in mind their important features. You will then be able to incorporate them in your gardens to harmonize with the site....

Arrange the stones fairly casually, not too precisely or skilfully....

When you want to dig out the pond and arrange stones there, you must determine the general layout of the pond, taking account of the structure of each part of the garden, you must decide on the shape of the pond and the position of the island. In this way you will be able to define the *tayori*...you will be able to design the pond and lay out the island....

When designing the 'south garden' of a house, it must be 18 to 21 metres [59 to 69 feet] deep from the edge of the steps to the bank of the pond or river, 24 to 27 metres [78 to 88 feet] if the residence belongs to the imperial family. But you may alter these measurements if the house is not all that large, bearing in mind the size of the pond, particularly in the case of temples and shrines.

In positioning the island, take account of the general aspect of the south garden, the measurements of the lake and its scale....

By following the topography of the site and the shape of the lake you can build mountains and determine the *no suji* [*no*: field, *suji*: line]....

As a general rule, when positioning

the island in the pond you should follow Chinese tradition. The water comes from the *Seyriu*, the east, and should flow towards the *Byakko*, the west.

The top of the stone positioned at the end of the pond should be 12 to 15 cm [4¾ to 5¾ in.] below the fishing pavilion to regulate the water level.

Tall stones should not normally be used except around the waterfall...at one end of the island...and near the mountain.

and out to sea. Create an impression of waves, a few reefs, peninsulas.

When you suggest a river it must be reminiscent of the way dragons and snakes move along, with a rustling sound. Place the main stones at the curves.

Once the stones are arranged, one of them must dominate. Therein lies a secret: the other stones must form a slope. The river water hits the stones and they change direction. Each of them

You should not erect stones over one metre [3 feet] high.

You should not erect stones within one metre of the house, or the owner will not be able to stay there for long and the garden will deteriorate....

'Creating a marine, river or marshy landscape'

If you want a marine landscape, first create the seashore. Arrange the stones in a bold way. If the layout is irregular, untidy and rough they will evoke the crashing of the waves on to the beach

The Golden Pavilion (Kinkaku-ji) surrounded by a 'landscape garden', a plate from *The Book of Gardens in Kyōto*, published in 1830.

must be strong enough to withstand the current. The gradual reduction in the force of the current must be reflected, creating a *fuzei*, a slight poetic feeling....

For a marsh garden stones are not normally used and if they are it is only in a few places, but you can plant reeds and irises. In that case it is better to make a feature of the expanse of water

The course of the stream below the house is clearly visible on this 12th-century *emaki*.

rather than building an island. The water must not be visible as it flows in. The water is calm, so the inflow and outflow are not dramatic. The point where the water comes in should be hidden. It is very important to make it look as though the water is overflowing.

There is only one fundamental rule to be followed; follow your initial idea, then after that follow your heart....

'Mountain Island'. You can have several mountain islands, but they must be of different heights. You can plant them thickly with trees. You can have beaches at the foot of the mountain as in the Inland Sea. If you place several stones at the foot of the mountain it will look like a mountain seen from the sea.

'Field Island'. Use autumn grasses, not trees. On a large island you can draw two or three *no suji*, sometimes

with an arrangement of stones. You will need to arrange the stones to determine the overall structure and then the autumn grasses. If necessary you can add moss and sandy beaches.

Rules for watercourses

First of all you have to decide the direction from which the water is to flow. According to the documents, when the river comes from the north-west it will flow south and then west. That is what it normally does.

East to west is the general rule, not normally west to north. In the north-east section of the garden it is best to make the water flow from north to south, below the house. This purifies and removes bad influences.

In the curve is the dragon's stomach. The main part of the house has to be built in the dragon's stomach. There should be no buildings in its back.

The watercourse symbolizes the emperor's relationship with his people. The earth is the emperor, the watercourse is the people. The water follows the earth's orders. If the earth stops the water, the water obeys. The water is all-powerful, the mountain is weak. The water can destroy the mountain....

Combinations of stones

Choose a large number of stones, large and small, and take them to the garden. After that the 'standing' stones have to be erected and the 'lying' stones placed flat according to their natural appearance. Decide which are the top and bottom and which the back and front of the stone. When you have decided that you can arrange the most important stones around the garden....

When you are arranging stones at the foot of the mountain, use plenty of stones to bear the weight of the mountain (visual weight).

When you are arranging the section of the garden, the stones should not be too tall. Arrange them as if they had been forgotten....

Taboos when erecting stones

If you disregard these taboos the owner of the house will fall ill, the house will fall into ruins and demons will arrive.

Examples of taboos:

You must not place upright a stone that was originally lying down. You must not lay down a stone that was originally upright. If you break these rules, you will be violating the spirit of the stone and harm will come to your family. If you place upright a stone that was originally lying down, you must not point it towards the house, even if it is some distance away. The stone would then become a source of harm.

You must not erect stones over one metre twenty or one metre fifty [4 to 5 feet] to the north-east of the house. If you do, the family will not live there for long. But nothing bad will happen to you if you place a *sari zon seki* to the south-west of the house....

The axes for positioning the stones must not coincide with the axes of the posts. If you break this taboo your descendants will be struck by misfortune and riches will elude you....

These taboos are not superstition; they are fundamental elements of the garden.

Extracts from the *Sakutei-ki*, 12th century

Arrangement of stones in *The Book of Gardens* by Rikoku Akizato, 1859.

Women's writing and travellers' tales

Japanese literature was born behind the movable screens of the rooms in the Heiankyō palaces. The women courtiers spent hours there, observing the courtesans' movements, conversations and intrigues. While men were still writing in Chinese characters, educated women transformed their language — the language of everyday life — into a lively and poetic idiom rich in imagery and began to record their impressions in Japanese kana characters. The themes of Murasaki Shikibu's Genji monogatari (illustrated here) have run like a thread throughout Japanese culture ever since.

The *Genji monogatari*

Murasaki Shikibu, the first woman writer in Japan produced the Genji monogatari, *a roman-fleuve about the imperial prince and his court, in the 11th century. Nature is the background to many of the episodes in the book and plants, rain and the passing of the seasons play an important part in the narrative.*

The Festival of the Cherry Blossoms

The festivities ended late in the night.

The courtiers went their ways, the empress and the crown prince departed, all was quiet. The moon came out more brightly. It wanted proper appreciation, thought Genji. The ladies in night attendance upon the emperor would be

asleep. Expecting no visitors, his own lady might have left a door open a crack. He went quietly up to her apartments, but the door of the one whom he might ask to show him in was tightly closed. He sighed. Still not ready to give up, he made his way to the gallery by Kokiden's pavilion. The third door from the north was open. Kokiden herself was with the emperor, and her rooms were almost deserted. The hinged door at the far corner was open too. All was silent. It was thus, he thought, that a lady invited her downfall. He slipped across the gallery and up to the door of the main room and looked inside. Everyone seemed to be asleep.

'What can compare with a misty moon of spring?' It was a sweet young voice, so delicate that its owner could be no ordinary serving woman.

She came (could he believe it?) to the door. Delighted, he caught at her sleeve.

'Who are you?' She was frightened.

'There is nothing to be afraid of.

"Late in the night we enjoy a misty moon.

There is nothing misty about the bond between us." '

Heartvine

Gentians and wild carnations peeped from the frosty tangles. After Tō no Chūjō had left, Genji sent a small bouquet by the little boy's nurse, Saishō, to Princess Omiya, with this message:

'Carnations at the wintry hedge remind me

Of an autumn which we leave too far behind.

Do you not think them a lovely colour?'

The Wormwood Patch

The safflower princess had lived a very straitened life after the death of her father, Prince Hitachi. Then had come that windfall. For Genji it had been the merest trifle, but for her, whose sleeves were so pitifully narrow, it was as if all the stars had suddenly fallen into her bowl. And then had come the days when the whole world had seemed to turn against him. Genji did not have time for everyone, and after his removal to distant Suma he did not or could not take the trouble to write. The princess wept for a time and lived a loveless and

threadbare existence after the tears had dried.

'Some people seem to have done all the wrong things in their other lives,' grumbled one of her old women. 'As if he had not been unkind enough already, the Blessed One all of a sudden brings a bit of pleasure – rather more than a bit, actually – and then takes it away again. How nice it was! The way of the world, you might say, that it should all disappear – and a body is expected to go on living.'

Yes, it had been very perverse of the Blessed One. A lady grows used to hunger and deprivation, but when they have been absent for a time they no longer seem like proper and usual conditions. Women who could be useful to her had somehow of their own accord come into her ken, and one by one they went away again; and so, as the months passed, her house was lonelier and lonelier.

Her gardens, never well tended, now offered ample cover for foxes and other sinister creatures, and owls hooted in unpruned groves morning and night. Tree spirits are shy of crowds, but when people go away they come forward as if claiming sovereignty. Frightening apparitions were numberless.

Murasaki Shikibu,
Genji monogatari (*The Tale of Genji*),
11th century,
translated by Edward G.
Seidensticker, 1976

The Pillow Book of Sei Shōnagon

Sei Shōnagon, another female writer of the Heian period, is famous for her Pillow Book, *in which even the commonplace has poetic significance.*

30. Things that Arouse a Fond Memory of the Past

A woman writer at Genji's court. Illustration for the *Genji monogatari*, 16th century.

Dried hollyhock.

The objects used during the Display of the Dolls.

To find a piece of deep violet or grape-coloured material that has been pressed between the pages of a notebook.

It is a rainy day and one is feeling bored. To pass the time, one starts looking through some old papers. And then one comes across the letters of a man one used to love.

Last year's paper fan.

A night with a clear moon.

44. Elegant Things

A white coat worn over a violet waistcoat.

Duck eggs.

Shaved ice mixed with liana syrup and put in a new silver bowl.

A rosary of rock crystal.

Snow on wisteria or plum blossoms.

A pretty child eating strawberries.

153. Squalid Things

The back of a piece of embroidery.

The inside of a cat's ear.

A swarm of mice, who still have no

fur, when they come wriggling out of their nest.

The seams of a fur robe that has not yet been lined.

Darkness in a place that does not give the impression of being very clean.

A rather unattractive woman who looks after a large brood of children.

A woman who falls ill and remains unwell for a long time. In the mind of her lover, who is not particularly devoted to her, she must appear rather squalid.

166. *Things that are Distant though Near*

Festivals celebrated near the Palace.

Relations between brothers, sisters, and other members of a family who do not love each other.

The zigzag path leading up to the temple at Kurama.

The last day of the Twelfth Month and the first of the First.

167. *Things that are Near though Distant*

Paradise.

The course of a boat.

Relations between a man and a woman.

Sei Shōnagon
The Pillow Book of Sei Shōnagon,
translated by Ivan Morris, 1979

The Journal of Sarashina

This book, contemporary with the two previous works, is notable for being the first travel journal, a new literary genre later adopted by monks and poets.

The Kiyomi barrier is by the sea. The guard post has several buildings and a palisade stretches into the sea. The spray seems to mingle with the smoke; how tall the waves at the Kiyomi barrier must be! The countryside is ravishingly beautiful. On the Tago shore the waves are high and we sail round them in a small boat. We find a ford on the Oi river. It is a strange river, white as if it had been mixed with thick flour, the water fast-flowing.

The Fujigawa is a river that gushes down Mount Fuji. A local inhabitant approaches us and tells us this story: 'On a very hot day last year I was just going about my business when I halted on the river bank and saw a yellowish object coming from upstream. I pulled it in and caught hold of it and I saw that it was an old document. When I picked it up I could see traces of elegant handwriting in red ink on the yellowing paper. I looked at it in astonishment. It was a list of all the provinces where posts were to be filled the following year. For this province, where there was to be a vacancy next year, it showed the name of the governor appointed and a second name. Surprised and intrigued, I took the document, dried it and kept it. The appointment the following year was exactly as written on the document. The governor of this province died within three months and his successor was the very person whose name had appeared next to his. That was the curious experience I had! I suppose they must be next year's appointments and all the gods who live on the mountain draw up the list the year before. It is certainly astonishing!' That was the story he told us....

On the 13th of the same month it was a cloudless moonlit night and about midnight, when everyone was asleep, we went to sit on the promenade. My older sister looked pensively at the moon. 'How would you feel if I vanished and left no trace?', she asked me. But seeing my horrified look she changed the subject and laughed. At that point we heard a cart nearby, with runners in front of it. It stopped and a voice called out, 'Reed leaf, reed leaf,' but no one answered. Tired of calling, the person played a very pretty tune on a clear-toned flute and finally continued on his way.

I said:

The sound of the flute
like the autumn wind
comes up in the night
why does reed leaf
not join in with her murmuring

and my sister agreed:

Without even waiting
until the reed leaf
could answer him
he went on his way
cruel was the sound of his flute.

And so we stayed there all night, gazing at the sky, and we did not go to bed until dawn.

The Journal of Sarashina, 11th century

The 18th century: travellers' tales

The Tokaido highway was not the only road to inspire painters and writers. Jakūchū describes the trip he made in a boat with a companion. As well as meditating on the natural surroundings of their retreat, the poets Bashō and Issa donned their straw hats, picked up their sticks and joined the itinerant monks on the roads of this 'ephemeral world'.

The Records of a Travel-worn Satchel

Matsuo Bashō:
'Abreast I am at last
With the fleeting spring
Here in the open bay
of Wakanoura.'

Dragging my sore heels, I plodded along like Saigyō, all the time with the memory of his suffering at the River Tenryū in my mind, and when I hired a horse, I thought of the famous priest who had experienced the disgrace of being thrown from his horse into a moat. Nevertheless, it was a great pleasure to see the marvellous beauties of nature, rare scenes in the mountains or along the coast, or to visit the sites of temporary abodes of ancient sages where they had spent secluded lives, or better

Sketch by Nanzan, painter, traveller and poet (above). Opposite: Bashō.

still, to meet people who had entirely devoted themselves to the search for artistic truth. Since I had nowhere permanent to stay, I had no interest whatever in keeping treasures, and since I was empty-handed, I had no fear of being robbed on the way. I walked at full ease, scorning the pleasure of riding in a palanquin, and filled my hungry stomach with coarse food, shunning the luxury of meat. I bent my steps in whatever direction I wished, having no itinerary to follow. My only mundane concerns were whether I would be able to find a suitable place to sleep at night and whether the straw sandals were the right size for my feet. Every turn of the road brought me new thoughts and every sunrise gave me fresh emotions. My joy was great when I encountered anyone with the slightest understanding of artistic elegance. Even those whom I had long hated for being antiquated and stubborn sometimes proved to be pleasant companions on my wandering journey. Indeed, one of the greatest pleasures of travelling was to find a genius hidden among weeds and bushes, a treasure lost in broken tiles, a mass of gold buried in clay, and when I did find such a person, I always kept a record in the hope that I might be able to show it to my friends.

Matsuo Bashō (1644–94)
The Narrow Road to the Deep North and other Travel Sketches, translated by Nobuyuki Yuasa, 1966

The Narrow Road to the Deep North

At the age of forty-five, 'the age at which a man who has lived and toiled so much feels his life drawing to a natural close', Bashō set off on a long pilgrimage north to the 'deep north', the very edge of the civilized world.

Days and months are travellers of eternity. So are the years that pass by. Those who steer a boat across the sea, or drive a horse over the earth till they succumb to the weight of years, spend every minute of their lives travelling. There are a great number of ancients, too, who died on the road. I myself have been tempted for a long time by the cloud-moving wind – filled with a strong desire to wander.

It was only towards the end of last autumn that I returned from rambling along the coast. I barely had time to sweep the cobwebs from my broken house on the River Sumida before the New Year, but no sooner had the spring mist begun to rise over the field than I wanted to be on the road again to cross the barrier-gate of Shirakawa in due time. The gods seemed to have possessed my soul and turned it inside out, and roadside images seemed to invite me from every corner, so that it was impossible for me to stay idle at home. Even while I was getting ready, mending my torn trousers, tying a new strap to my hat, and applying *moxa* to my legs to strengthen them, I was already dreaming of the full moon rising over the islands of Matsushima. Finally, I sold my house, moving to the cottage of Sampū for a temporary stay....

I walked all through that day, ever wishing to return after seeing the strange sights of the far north, but not really believing in the possibility, for I knew that departing like this on a long journey in the second year of Genroku I should only accumulate more frosty hairs on my head as I approached the colder regions. When I reached the village of Sōka in the evening, my bony shoulders were sore because of the load I had carried, which consisted of a paper coat to keep me warm at night, a light cotton gown to wear after the bath, scanty protection against the rain, writing equipment, and gifts from certain friends of mine. I wanted to travel light, of course, but there were always certain things I could not throw away for either practical or sentimental reasons.

Matsuo Bashō, *The Narrow Road to the Deep North and other Travel Sketches*, translated by Nobuyuki Yuasa, 1966

Zen poetry and art

Different forms of poetry have evolved over the centuries. The most ancient, the waka, *dates back to the 8th century. The oldest anthology of poetry still in existence is the* Manyōshū. *The* haiku, *a major poetic genre, appeared later and has survived to the present day. Several prominent Zen monks, such as Sengai and Hakuin, were also poets and travellers.*

Painting and early Zen teaching

Paintings often reflect the ways in which Zen teachings may connect the visual with the poetic. Many paintings contain Zen inscriptions.

Vibrating within
the ear are many voices
but their origin
has a source which may be called
the sound of no sound
> Takuan (1573–1645)
> in Stephen Addiss,
> *The Art of Zen: Paintings and Calligraphy by Japanese Monks 1600–1925*, 1989

My banishment
has been ended, and I think
I'd like to return –
but I don't much like Edo,
the hub of the squalid world
> Takuan, *Ibid.*

This old monk meditates and rests in the empty mountains
In loneliness and stillness through the days and nights.

Calligraphy by Takuan.

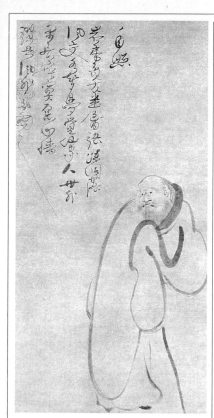

Self-enlightenment by Fūgai.

What moon is white, and wind high?
His life is just this chant of meditation.

How can he smile so happily?
Do not compare him with others;
His worldliness is not worldly,
His joy comes from his own nature.

Who in the world can discuss him,
With his oversize body full of good luck.
How laughable – this old guest
Is the only one travelling the road.

> Fūgai, *Ibid.*

Breathing in, breathing out,
Moving forward, moving back,
Living, dying, coming, going –
Like two arrows meeting in flight,
In the midst of nothingness
There is a road that goes directly to my
    true home.

> Gesshū (1618–96), *Ibid.*

Holding his staff, he points out
That humans were originally without
    form,
Otherwise, true form could not be
    formed.
Benevolent people are naturally
    humane,
For if you suddenly understand and
    abide in the teachings,
You begin to understand that
    discriminations are empty.

> Mokuan (1611–84), *Ibid.*

When I leave the pure cliffs, I am
    distracted by callers –
The world of men is first and always the
    world of men.

> Fūgai (1568–1654), *Ibid.*

His life is not poor,
He has riches beyond measure.
Pointing to the moon, gazing at the
    moon,
This old guest follows the way.

> Fūgai, *Ibid.*

The revival of Zen teaching: painting, calligraphy, humour

In the 18th century two monks, Hakuin and Sengai, revived the teaching of Zen through painting and calligraphy, using humour to show that the mind is outside the world of forms and that nothing is fixed.

The Meditating Frog

If a man becomes a Buddha by just
  practising *zazen*,
Mean frog though I am I should have
  been one long before this!

Sengai (1750–1837)

Zazen means 'sitting in meditation'. The
frog seems to be always in this posture
when we find him in the garden. If the
meditation posture alone constitutes
Zen the frog's attainment of Buddha-
hood must be an event taking place a
long time before. But Zen is more than
mere sitting. There must be an
awakening in the unconscious.

Kokusai Bunka Shinkokai, *Sengai,
Catalogue of Travelling
Exhibition in Europe*, 1961

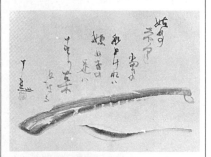

Above: *The Ladle and the Pestle* by Sengai.
Top: *The Meditating Frog* by Sengai.

The Ladle and the Pestle

When the mother-in-law's ladle is too
  severely in use,
The daughter-in-law's legs become
  stiff like a pestle.

Sengai

The mother-in-law is
traditionally hard on her
son's wife, the newly
adopted one to the family.
The latter is mercilessly
ordered about too frequently
and too severely by the
matron of her new home.
Trying to carry out her orders
the young wife has to do
much moving from one place
  to another,

and finally her legs give
  out – they turn into a
  stiff pair of sticks, like a
  surikogi. A *surikogi* is a
  big wooden pestle used in
  the kitchen.

Kokusai Bunka Shinkokai,
*Sengai, Catalogue of Travelling
Exhibition in Europe*, 1961

The monkey tries to catch hold of the
moon in the water.

He will not give up until death gets
    the better of him.
If only he does not let go of the branch
    and fall into the deep pool
The whole world would shine with
    a dazzling light!

                Hakuin (1685–1768)

The world of the *haiku*

The haiku *is a brief expression of transient
enlightenment in which we see the living
reality of objects. Buson, Issa and Bashō
are amongst the best-known* haiku *poets.
In the example below, Bashō finds
enlightenment as he listens to the sound of
a frog jumping into a pond.*

Ah! How still the pond!
Abruptly a frog leaps in:
The sound of water!

              Bashō (1644–94)
    Shadowless Ants, the Book of Haikus

As I ride my horse
Through cold rice-fields my shadow
Creeps along the ground.

              Bashō, *Ibid.*

It wraps its being
In the sweet-potato leaf
The drop of water.

        Kikaku (1660–1707), *Ibid.*

Winter plum, your limbs
Are twisted and creak. Like mine,
Ancient as I am.

        Buson (1715–83), *Ibid.*

With my single tooth
I bite on the frozen brush
In the dark of night.

             Buson, *Ibid.*

Soft breeze of evening
The stream parts and flows around
The blue heron's feet.

             Buson, *Ibid.*

Calligraphy and portrait of a poet by
Buson, 18th century. Opposite:
A Monkey by Hakuin.

When the west wind blows
Taking refuge in the east
Are the fallen leaves.

             Buson, *Ibid.*

Competing with me
To make the other blink first
Is the staring frog.

        Issa (1763–1827), *Ibid.*

Amorous moanings
From my tortoise, you bemuse
These simple peasants.

        Kyoshi (1874–1959), *Ibid.*

On the still surface
Of a water jar there floats
A shadowless ant.

          Seishi (1901), *Ibid.*

Printmaking

In the 18th century the Japanese print reflected a society in which art was an expression of freedom. Prints continue to be made today in old wooden houses in Tokyo, where the workshops are still the same as they were two hundred years ago. The craftsmen use the same techniques and skills as their predecessors, taking some of their subjects from Hiroshige and Hokusai but also creating 'woodcuts' for contemporary artists.

Japanese prints are made not from an engraving but by cutting into a block of wood. The artist's outline of all the lines and surfaces to be printed on the paper is first transferred to a cherry wood block. Cherry wood is used because it stands up to the pressure of repeated printing but is at the same time flexible enough for both large flat surfaces and very fine lines to be carved into it. In the transfer the original drawing is placed on the wood and 'destroyed' in the cutting process. This stage can only be carried out by very experienced artists. The creation of the print (a unique art form completely different from a drawing or painting) relies on their skill and sensitivity and so does its preservation. It can be reproduced, but because of its spontaneity it is inimitable.

A wood block for each colour

At least one block is cut for each colour. More than one application is needed to achieve the glossy intensity of the black or the patterns that appear in it, the characteristics of some blues or the green or yellow. The only guide is a gouge

Stage one: carving on wood.

mark or a relief right angle (*kentō*). In the next stage the printer will use this to position the paper on each of the wood blocks in turn, in a very precise order (the blocks having first been coated with the appropriate colour). It needs a steady hand and eye and considerable skill to make the lines sharp and to juxtapose the colours without any smearing or white gaps. In the printing process the front is against the wood block, which has been coated with colour, and the colour is rubbed into the paper with a pad (*baren*) covered with a bamboo leaf. This concentric and firm movement often leaves traces on the back of the print. Sometimes the marks of the block with which the print has been in contact during the printing process are also visible on the front of the print itself.

Mulberry bark paper

The paper is made from mulberry bark, pounded, crushed to a pulp and mixed with vegetable size. This process makes it flexible, allowing the ink to penetrate easily, and dense, so that the colours do not spread. It is often possible to tell from the feel and sound of the paper what prints were originally like in each period. The paper is always basically the same but various types and thicknesses were used by different artists and in different periods. The print appears in several traditional formats and there is a reason for each of them, depending on the artist's inspiration and the tastes of art lovers as well as the restrictions imposed by the nature of the wood. The signature and seal of the artist or the publisher's or censor's seal (sometimes all three) appear on the finished print. The names of the woodcutter and printer (at the publisher's workshop) are not normally shown. They remain anonymous, even though they have contributed equally to the production of the finished work. Nor is there any indication of the number of prints or the position of the work in the series. Because of the characteristics of the wood, the number of standard prints that can be run off without alteration in the 'first print run' is generally reckoned to be about three hundred. However, with some commissions from 'societies' it might be as few as ten and in some cases only one copy of a print is known to exist.

Nelly Delay

In 1795 Utamaro portrayed his 'famous beauties' engraving and making prints (above), an activity normally reserved for men.

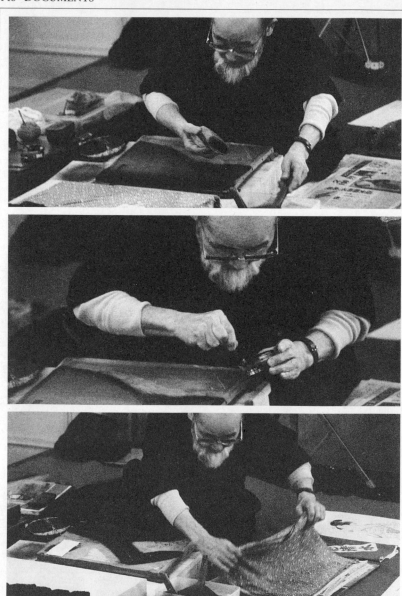

Traditional printing processes: coating the wood (opposite above and opposite centre), taking a sheet of paper kept wet (opposite bottom), placing it carefully on the wood using the *kentō* guide mark (top), pressing the paper on the wood and turning with the *baren* (above centre), lifting the printed sheet gently to avoid smudging (above).

Hokusai

Hokusai, a genius 'obsessed with drawing', occupies a unique place in Japanese art. Although his Wave *fascinated the West and inspired Debussy, he himself was attracted to the western sciences taught by the Dutch on the island of Deshima. His research was influenced by his visits there and perspective, anatomy and botany all make an appearance in the* Mangwa. *At the same time he retained a deep attachment to Zen and had an insatiable curiosity for every aspect of the 'ephemeral' world.*

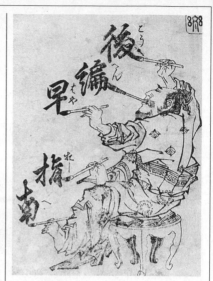

A humorous self-portrait by Hokusai in the frontispiece of *Brief Introduction to Simplified Drawing*, 1812.

Hokusai discussed his ideas on the art of painting and drawing in his letters and in the introductions to some of his books.

On printmaking

In an undated letter to the publisher Kobayashi, Hokusai wrote:

In the light tones of the Chinese ink I do not use any shading, because although it is easy for the painter working with a brush the craftsman who prints the plates can make barely two hundred shaded copies; it is impossible to make more than that on the same wood block. And make the shade of the light-coloured ink as light as possible. If it is darker it does not look attractive when it is printed. Tell the craftsman that the light-coloured ink has to be the colour of shellfish soup, in other words very light.

Now, for the shade of the medium-dark ink, if it is printed too light it makes the colour not so strong and the craftsman must be told that the medium-dark colour has to be quite thick, rather like bean soup. I shall in any case look at the samples but I am making these suggestions straight away because I want my drawings to be 'properly cooked'.

Hokusai often added a postscript to his letters and he went on:

I would suggest that the engraver does not add the eyelid below when I do not draw it; these two noses are mine [*drawing of a nose, side and front view*] and the ones they usually engrave are Utagawa noses that I do not like at all and that do not conform to the rules of drawing. It is also fashionable to draw eyes like this [*drawings of eyes with a mirror painted black in the centre*], but I do not like these eyes any more than the noses.

On painting methods

In How to Draw with a Compass and Ruler, *Hokusai discusses colours and 'how to see the proportions of objects'.*

The colours must not be too thick or too light and the brush must be flat, otherwise it makes things dirty; the colouring water light rather than dark, because it would harden the tone; the line never too sharp, but with a pronounced shading; only use the colour after letting it sit for a while and after removing the dust that has risen to the surface; the colour must be dissolved with the finger and never the brush; only put the colour on the black lines of the shade, that is the only place the colour can be added....

There is old black and fresh black, glossy black and matt black, black in the light and black in the shade. For old black you have to mix in red; for fresh black, blue; for matt black, white; for glossy black, you add size; black in the light needs a grey reflection....

In the old days it used to be said that a mountain is made ten feet high, trees one foot, horses an inch, people as big as a bean and that was declared to be the rule of proportion in art. No, lines in a drawing consist of circles and squares.... Now I, Hokusai, have taken a ruler and compass and have used them to draw everything so that I could determine the shape accurately. It is a little like the old method of feeling your way with a piece of charcoal [a piece of burnt wood]. Anyone who learns to handle the ruler and compass properly will be able to make the finest and most delicate drawings.

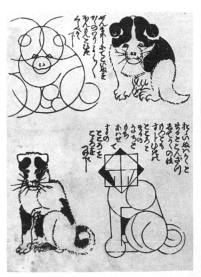

A page from *How to Draw with a Compass and Ruler.*

Short cuts to drawing

In his Brief Introduction to Simplified Drawing, *published in 1812, Hokusai explains brush technique and the calligraphic simplification of shapes (relationship of words to pictures) as well as the geometrical breakdown of shapes into circles and squares.*

running away from the paper. Is that not truly extraordinary? A publisher who was told about this asked for the drawings in such a way that I could not refuse. Fortunately the engraver Ko-Izoumi, a very skilful woodcarver, undertook to cut the veins and nerves of the figures I drew with his well-sharpened knife and managed to deprive

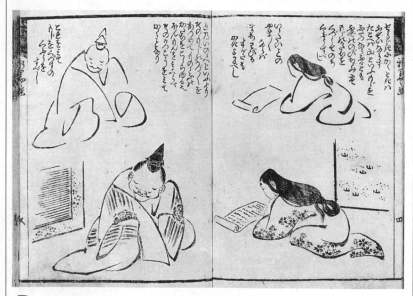

Plate from Hokusai's *Brief Introduction to Simplified Drawing*, 1812.

The painter Yama mizou Tengou, of Noshi-Koshi yama, liked the pretentious style of Hema-mou-sho-Niudō and adopted his incomprehensible style of drawing. I have studied the style myself for nearly a hundred years and have not understood it any more than he did, but something curious did happen to me: I found that my figures, my animals, insects and fish, looked as if they were

them of their freedom to run away....

People have copied the shapes of things since ancient times. They took the sun, moon and stars from the sky, the mountains, trees, fish and then houses and fields from the earth and these simplified, altered and denatured images have become characters in writing. But anyone claiming to be an artist has to respect the original shapes of things and when he designs houses, palaces or temples it is absolutely essential that he should understand their underlying structure.

An architect wrote a book called *Architectural Models*. My publisher asked me to illustrate the second volume. The first was illustrated by an architectural expert, with technical data. What I have done with this volume is more artistic, but if, thanks to my teaching, young artists are successful in not drawing a cat instead of a tiger, a *tombi* instead of a falcon, even if my work is just a pebble beside a mountain I shall be proud of what I have achieved for posterity....

This book is not just for children; it will help adults, poets for instance, who want to make a quick drawing in a society. It is an introduction to cursive drawing.

At the end of the book Hokusai adds:

I was inspired to write this book when Yū-yū Kiwan [curious name] asked me at home one evening how you could learn to draw quickly and easily. I told him the best way was a game in which you try and form drawings from letters and I took my brush and showed him how easy it was to draw. After I had done two or three drawings, the publisher Kōshodō, who was present at the time, did not want the drawings to be lost and he asked me to design a whole book, which must essentially be seen as a hobby or diversion for passing the time.

'Nothing I produced before the age of seventy really counts'

In 1835 the master made an astonishing revelation in the introduction to a Hundred Views of Mount Fuji.

Since the age of six I have been obsessed with drawing the shapes of things. By the time I was about fifty I had published countless drawings, but nothing I produced before the age of seventy really counts. It was not until I was seventy-three that I more or less understood the real structure of nature, of animals, grasses, trees, birds, fish and insects.

So by the time I am eighty I shall have progressed even further; by the time I am ninety I shall penetrate the mystery of objects; by the time I reach the age of a hundred I shall certainly have become some kind of prodigy; and when I am a hundred and ten everything I do, whether a point or a line, will be alive. I want those who live as long as I do to see if I keep my word. Written at the age of seventy-five by me, formerly Hokusai, now Gwakiō Rōjin, the old man obsessed with drawing.

Hokusai, quoted by Edmond de Goncourt, in *Hokusai*, 1984

Facsimile of the portrait of Hokusai in his eighties, painted by his daughter Oyei.

CHRONOLOGY

YAMATO PERIOD

End of 4th century The Yamato court (*Yamato-chōtei*) unifies Japan
538 Introduction of Buddhism
587 Clan warfare; Mononobe clan defeated by Soga clan
592 Shōtoku Taishi, regent of Japan, declares Buddhism the state religion
604 Constitution in Seventeen Articles (*Jūshichi jō kempō*)

ASUKA PERIOD

672 *Jinshin no ran*: civil war of imperial succession
689 Code of Asuka no Kiyomihara

NARA PERIOD

710 Capital established in Nara (Heijōkyō)
720 Official date of *Nihonshoki* (history of Japan's origins)
743 Newly cleared land from now on became private property
749 Great Buddha built at Tōdai-ji
790 Compilation of *Manyōshū* (first anthology of poetry)

HEIAN PERIOD

794 Capital moved to Kyōto (Heiankyō)
805 Saichō returns from Tang China and establishes the Tendai sect in Japan
816 Kūkai returns from Tang China and establishes the Shingon sect in Japan
894 Sugawara no Michizane stops diplomatic missions to China
Early 11th century The *Genji monogatari*, the first novel in Japanese, is written by Lady Murasaki Shikibu
1022 Fujiwara no Michinaga, who established the Fujiwara clan as supreme leaders, formally dedicates the Hōjō-ji temple he has had built
1180 Minamoto no Yoritomo marshals troops in Izu and enters Kamakura

KAMAKURA PERIOD

1192 Minamoto no Yoritomo becomes *shōgun*
1232 Hōjō Yasutoki promulgates the *Jōei shikimoku* laying down the legal rules and principles of the Kamakura government
1274 and **1281** Mongol invasions

1333 End of Kamakura *bakufu*
1336 Dynastic schism between 'Northern and Southern Dynasties'

MUROMACHI PERIOD

1368 Ashikaga Yoshimitsu, the third *shōgun* of that name, defeats rival clans and establishes the rule of the Ashikaga
1392 Northern and Southern Dynasties united; end of dynastic schism
1397 After abdicating and becoming a monk, Ashikaga Yoshimitsu has the Kinkaku-ji (Golden Pavilion) built
1428 Peasant revolts
1467 Beginning of Onin civil war over *shōgun* succession, a power struggle between the *daimyō*
1473 Ginkaku-ji (Silver Pavilion) built for Ashikaga Yoshimasa
1495 Hōjō Sōun takes Odawara castle. Beginning of the 'Warring Kingdoms' period
1543 The Portuguese land at Kanegashima. From them the Japanese obtain their first firearms, which later transformed military architecture
1549 Francis Xavier begins preaching
1573 Oda Nobunaga deposes Ashikaga Yoshiaki. End of Muromachi *bakufu*

AZUCHI-MOMOYAMA PERIOD

1580 Nobunaga places the Honganji monks under supervision, curtailing the military and secular power of the Buddhist monasteries
1582 Nobunaga assassinated. Toyotomi Hideyoshi comes to power
1583 Hideyoshi has a castle built in Osaka, on the Hongan-ji site
1587 Hideyoshi bans Christianity
1588 Disarmament of rural areas. Only nobles are allowed to bear arms
1590 Hideyoshi reunifies the country
1594 Hideyoshi has Momoyama castle built
1598 Death of Hideyoshi
1600 Tokugawa Ieyasu takes over power from other *daimyōs* after the battle of Sekigahara

EDO PERIOD

1603–16 Shogunate of Tokugawa Ieyasu
1615 Tokugawa Ieyasu besieges the Toyotomi castle at Osaka and defeats the last supporters of Hideyoshi
1622 Fifty-five Christians killed in Nagasaki

1636 Ports closed to foreigners
1637 Shimabara revolt by Christians after Christianity is banned in Japan
1641 Dutch settle at Deshima
1657 Great fire of Edo
1673 Restriction on parcelling out of land
1732 and 1783 Great famines

1853 Commodore Perry's ships anchor at Uraga in the bay of Edo
1854 Treaty of Kanagawa opens the ports of Shimoda and Hakodate to trade with America
1864 Western ships bombard Shimonoseki
1867 End of Tokugwa *bakufu*
1868 Beginning of Meiji period

FURTHER READING

Addiss, Stephen, *The Art of Zen: Paintings and Calligraphy by Japanese Monks 1600–1925,* 1989

Bechert, Heinz, and Richard Gombrich (eds.), *The World of Buddhism,* 1984

Blomberg, Catharina, *The Heart of the Warrior: Origins and Religious Background of the Samurai System in Feudal Japan,* 1994

Clark, Timothy, *Ukiyo-e Paintings in the British Museum,* 1992

Delay, Nelly, *L'Estampe japonaise,* 1993

—, *Japan-Occident, Les Sources japonaises de l'art occidental,* 1986

—, *Les Natures mortes dans les estampes surimono,* vol. 1: *Les Objets tranquilles,* 1978; vol. 2: *La Voix silencieuse des choses,* 1988

de Sabato Swinton, Elizabeth, *The Women of the Pleasure Quarter: Japanese Paintings and Prints of the Floating World,* 1995

Ernst, Earle, *The Kabuki Theatre,* 1974

Henderson, Harold G., *The Bamboo Broom: An Introduction to Haiku,* 1934

Hibbett, Howard, *The Floating World in Japanese Fiction,* 1975

Hillier, Jack, *The Art of the Japanese Book,* 1987

— *Japanese Colour Prints,* 1991

— *Hokusai: Paintings, Drawing and Woodcuts,* 1978

— *Suzuki Harunobu: An Exhibition of his Colour Prints and Illustrated Books on the Occasion of the Bicentenary of his Death,* 1970

— *Utamaro: Colour Prints and Paintings,* 1961

Keene, Donald, *Nō: The Classical Theatre of Japan,* 1966

King, Winston L., *Zen and the Way of the Sword: Arming the Samurai Psyche,* 1993

Kitagawa, Joseph M., *On Understanding Japanese Religion,* 1987

Lane, Richard, *Images for the Floating World: The Japanese Print,* 1978

Michener, James A., *The Hokusai Sketchbooks: Selections from the Manga,* 1996

Morris, Ivan, *The World of the Shining Prince: Court Life in Ancient Japan,* 1976

Morse, Peter, *Hokusai: One Hundred Poets,* 1989

Rambach, Pierre and Suzanne, *Le Livre secret des jardins japonais,* 1973

Robinson, Basil William, *Kuniyoshi,* 1982

Russell Robinson, Henry, *Japanese Arms and Armour,* 1969

Shimizu, Yoshiaki (ed.), *Japan: The Shaping of Daimyō Culture, 1185–1868,* 1989

Slawson, David A., *Secret Teachings in the Art of Japanese Gardens: Design Principles, Aesthetic Values,* 1987

Stanley-Baker, Joan, *Japanese Art,* 1984

Tanaka, Sen'ō, *The Tea Ceremony,* 1982

Treat Paine, Robert, and Alexander Soper, *The Art and Architecture of Japan,* 1974

Ueda, Makoto, *Bashō and his Interpreters: Selected Hokku with Commentary,* 1991

Watson, William (ed.), *The Great Japan Exhibition: Art of the Edo Period 1600–1868,* 1981

LIST OF ILLUSTRATIONS

The following abbreviations have been used:
a above; *b* below; *c* centre; *l* left; *r* right.

COVER

Front *Genji monogatari emaki* (detail), Suzumushi chapter. Painting, 12th century. Gotō Museum of Art, Tokyo
Spine A screen (detail). Musée Guimet, Paris
Back Zen garden (detail) at the Daitoku-ji, Kyōto

OPENING

INDEX

Page numbers in *italics* relate to illustrations or references in captions.

ACKNOWLEDGMENTS

The author wishes to express her gratitude to Paul Gottlieb for his faith in her and to Françoise Cachin. Thanks are also due to the following for their help and support: Anisabelle Beres, Laurent Berman, Colette Davaze, Neil Davey, Norbert Lagane, Georges Mann, Janette Ostier, Geoffrey Staines and Arthur Vershbow. The author and the publishers particularly wish to thank Frédéric Mazuy, Joseph Ziolo and, above all, Dominique Rivolier-Ruspoli for her invaluable help with the illustrations.

PHOTO CREDITS

AKG/Werner Forman 17c, 18–9, 64, 65, 69, 71, 72ar, 72br, 74–5b, 78–9, 96, 100. Artephot/Ogawa 25r, 26b, 28a, 29l, 30–1, 33r, 34, 35, 36, 37, 39, 40–1, 44–5, 45, 80–1. Artephot/Shobunsha 46. Artephot/Shogakukan 18, 21b, 22, 119l. Artephot/Zauto–Press 54a. Asukaen 27. British Library, London 105a. British Museum, London 70l, 143. Laurent Chastel 42, 43, 44, 50–1, 59, 60–1, 81, 114b, 115b, 117a, 117b, 129, 138. L. Christophe Collection 66–7. Dagli-Orti 24, 70r, 88–9. Nelly Delay 46–7, 52–3, 67, 83. Diaf/B.Simmons 28b. Edimedia 58–9. Eisi Bunko Museum, Tokyo 140, 142r. Enguerand/A. Pacciani 62–3. Explorer/R. Baumgartner 94b. Gallimard archives 74–5c, 76–7. Suzanne Held, Paris 4–5, 6, 7, 8–9, 54b, 56–7, 92b. Hoa Qui/S. Grandadam 12. Galerie Huguette Bérès, Paris 98. Idemitsu Museum of Arts, Tokyo 142al, 142bl. Magnum/R. Burri 94a. Magnum/B. Glinn 1. Magnum/T. Höpker 2. Photo Jean Mazenod, *L'Art de l'ancien Japon*, Editions Citadelles et Mazenod, Paris 85r. Pix/M. Trigalou 3. Private collection 52, 63, 131, 132, 141, 145, 151. Private collection, Japan 115a. Rapho/G. Sioen 14–5. Rapho/M. S. Yamashita 54–5, 80, 93. Réunion des Musées Nationaux spine, 15, 31, 100–1, 103b. RMN/Arnaudet 17a. RMN/R. Lambert 17b, 25l, 84. Dominique Rivolier-Ruspoli back cover, 11, 20a, 20b, 21a, 23, 32, 33l, 38l, 38r, 40, 50, 51, 53c, 53b, 56b, 57b, 62, 68, 68–9, 75, 76, 85l, 86al, 86r, 87l, 87r, 90, 91a, 91b, 92a, 95, 102, 103al, 104, 105b, 106–7, 106, 108, 109a, 109b, 110l, 110r, 111, 112b, 113, 114a, 116a, 116b, 118, 120, 121a, 121b, 122–3, 124–5, 126a, 126b, 127, 128, 133, 134, 135, 136, 139, 144, 146, 147, 148, 149, 150. Sheldan Comfert Collins 119r. Sotheby's, London 13, 41, 58, 72l, 73, 74, 82, 97, 99, 103cl, 103cr, 103r, 107, 112a. Toppan Art Mall/Goto Art Museum, Tokyo front cover, 48–9.

TEXT CREDITS

Grateful acknowledgment is made for use of material from the following works: (pp. 140–1) Reprinted from Stephen Addiss, *The Art of Zen: Paintings and Calligraphy by Japanese Monks 1600–1925*, Harry N. Abrams, Inc., 1989; © Stephen Addiss 1989; reprinted by permission of the author. (pp. 138–9) 4 lines and approximately 700 words (pp. 84–6, 97 and 99) from *The Narrow Road to the Deep North and other Travel Sketches* by Matsuo Bashō, translated by Nobuyuki Yuasa (Penguin Classics), 1966; copyright © Nobuyuki Yuasa, 1966; reproduced by permission of Penguin Books Ltd. (pp. 134–6) From *The Tale of Genji* by Murasaki Shikibu, trans. Edward G. Seidensticker, Martin Secker & Warburg, 1976; copyright © 1976 by Edward G. Seidensticker; reprinted by permission of Alfred A. Knopf, Inc., and Random House UK Limited, London. (pp. 136–7) From *The Pillow Book of Sei Shōnagon*, translated by Ivan Morris. Copyright © 1991 Columbia University Press; reprinted by permission of the publisher; reprinted by permission of Oxford University Press.

Nelly Delay
is a graduate of the Louvre school of art and
an art historian specializing in ancient Japanese art.
Between 1974 and 1987 she organized a number
of exhibitions, for which she wrote the catalogues, including
*Dessin japonais, Les Natures mortes japonaises au XVIIIe siècle,
Les Peintures de la cour du prince Genji* and *Japon-Occident*.
She is the author of *L'Estampe japonaise* (1993) and lectures
at the CNRS, OECD and various cultural organizations.

For Gabrielle

Translated from the French by Lorna Dale

For Harry N. Abrams, Inc.
Eve Sinaiko, editorial

Library of Congress Cataloging-in-Publication Data

Delay, Nelly.
    [Japon éternel. English]
    The art and culture of Japan / Nelly Delay
        p.   cm. — (Discoveries)
    Includes index.
    ISBN 0–8109–2862–0 (pbk.)
    1. Japan—Civilization.   I. Title.   II. Series: Discoveries (New
York, N.Y.)
    DS821.D456   1999
    952—dc21   99–24627

Printed and bound in Italy by Editoriale Lloyd, Trieste